Berlitz®

MW01709924

cuaderno de **inglés** *básico*

Lynne Strugnell

Berlitz Publishing/APA Publications GmbH & Co. Verlag KG, Singapore Branch, Singapore

Workbook series devised by Lynne Strugnell
Spanish Workbook written by Phil Turk
Handwriting font © Henry Bloomfield 1994

Impreso en Singapur por Insight Print Services (Pte) Ltd., enero 2005

CONTENIDOS

Introducción

Desde hace más de un siglo, a través de sus cursos y sus libros de idioma, Berlitz ha ayudado a millones de personas a aprender lenguas extranjeras para negocios, para viajes u otros intereses, concentrándose en el uso del lenguaje moderno e idiomático en la comunicación.

Este *Workbook de inglés Berlitz* ha sido diseñado para estudiantes que han aprendido suficiente inglés para mantener una conversación sencilla y que ahora desean mejorar sus conocimientos lingüísticos y aumentar la confianza en sí mismos.

Es posible que Ud. esté siguiendo algún curso nocturno o que Ud. sea autodidacta y desee tener más práctica en el idioma, o tal vez haya aprendido inglés hace tiempo y necesite estimular su habilidad lingüística. En cualquier caso, encontrará en el *Workbook de inglés Berlitz* una forma fácil y divertida de perfeccionar su inglés.

Cómo utilizar el Workbook.

Le recomendamos que se ponga como objetivo un tiempo de estudio semanal o diario que Ud. pueda cumplir con regularidad. Las unidades van progresando en nivel de dificultad y van siguiendo el desarrollo de una historia, por lo que probablemente Ud. querrá empezar por la Unidad 1.

Cada unidad enfoca algún tema o situación específicos: conocer gente nueva, presentarse, comer en un restaurante, los viajes, el ocio, y muchos más. En cada unidad encontrará Ud. ejercicios y juegos de palabras que enriquecerán su vocabulario, su gramática y su destreza comunicativa.

Los ejercicios varían, pero cada unidad sigue una misma secuencia básica:

Juegos de palabras	Ejercicios relativamente sencillos que presentan cada tema.
De persona a persona	Una variedad de ejercicios basados en diálogos idiomáticos muy divertidos. Lea estos diálogos con atención pues ellos presentan vocabulario y expresiones que Ud. utilizará en otros ejercicios.
El idioma en la mira	Práctica dirigida a solucionar dificultades gramaticales específicas.
Texto en contexto	Estimulantes ejercicios de comprensión, basados en textos cortos.
A escribir	Breves ejercicios de escritura y redacción que hacen uso del vocabulario clave y de la gramática de los ejercicios anteriores.

Hemos proporcionado espacios para que Ud. escriba sus respuestas en el *Workbook,* aunque, si así lo desea, tal vez prefiera Ud. escribir en una hoja por separado.

Si Ud. quiere verificar el sentido de una palabra, el glosario al final del libro le da su traducción al inglés. La sección de gramática le ofrece una útil perspectiva de las estructuras básicas que se cubren en este libro. Ud. puede verificar todas las respuestas en la clave.

Le deseamos mucha suerte con sus estudios, esperando que el *Workbook* le resulte útil y divertido a la vez.

UNIDAD 1: All about me

En la unidad 1 practicaremos cómo dar nuestro nombre y nuestra dirección, cómo presentarnos y cómo hablar sobre las diferentes nacionalidades.

Juegos de palabras

1. El verbo *to be*

Relacione las palabras del cuadro superior con la forma apropiada del verbo.

she I he it Mike they you we Mr. & Mrs. Thomas Liz and I

am is are

De persona a persona

2. Aprendamos a presentarnos

Esta mañana Bob Kushner tiene una entrevista para un nuevo empleo. Lea el diálogo y complete los espacios en blanco con una de las palabras que aparecen a continuación.

are	I'm	isn't	it's	meet	you

Bob	Good morning.
Betty	Good morning! Mr. Thomas?
Bob	No, my name __________ Thomas. __________ Kushner, Bob Kushner.
Betty	Oh, Mr. Kushner! __________ sorry! How do __________ do? I'm Betty Stones.
Bob	Pleased to __________ you, Ms. Stones.
Betty	Coffee? Tea?
Bob	Thank you. Coffee, please.
Betty	Sue! SUE!...SUE? Where __________ you?
Sue	Sorry! Yes?
Betty	Sue, one coffee and one tea, please.

Palabras mágicas

3. Países y nacionalidades

Complete el siguiente cuadro:

País	Nacionalidad
France	French
Spain	
England	
	Bolivian
	Cuban
Italy	
the United States	
	Canadian
Japan	
	Venezuelan
Colombia	

4. Los números

Ordene las letras para identificar los números. Una con una línea las palabras con los números correctos.

herte ______________

ixs ___six___

veens ______________

net ______________

wot ______________

eon ______________

enni ______________

rufo ______________

thige ______________

vief ______________

El idioma en la mira

5. Contracciones

Escriba las oraciones utilizando la contracción apropiada, como en el ejemplo.

Ejemplo: He is Mexican. He's Mexican.

1. His name is Bob Kushner. ______________________
2. They are from France. ______________________
3. What is your name? ______________________
4. I am Betty Stones. ______________________
5. We are American. ______________________
6. It is coffee. ______________________
7. She is my girlfriend. ______________________
8. Where is my coffee? ______________________

6. Formas negativas

Observe los dibujos y haga oraciones siguiendo el ejemplo. Utilice las contracciones verbales.

Ejemplo:

He isn't Mr. Kushner.

He's Mr. Thomas.

1. ______________________
She's Spanish.

2. ______________________
They're from Canada.

3. ______________________
It's tea.

4. Her name ______________________
It's James.

5. ______________________
I'm married.

Texto en contexto

7. Información personal

Estudie la información que aparece en la solicitud de empleo de Bob. Escriba la descripción en el orden correcto en el espacio en blanco.

married, he's single. He's
is American. He's from
Baltimore. She's 29 (twenty-nine).
28 River Street West. He isn't
Bob Kushner
Jane. She's from
Los Angeles. His address is
31 (thirty-one). His girlfriend's name is

¡A escribir!

8. ¿Quién soy yo?

Construya oraciones sobre Ud. mismo.

Ejemplo: (name) My name is Betty Stones.

Personal Information

(name) ---

(address) ---

(nationality) ---

(age) ---

(married/single) ---

UNIDAD 2: I've got a new job.

En la Unidad 2 hablaremos sobre nuestra familia, preguntaremos la edad de los demás y hablaremos sobre su trabajo.

Juegos de palabras

1. Preguntas y respuestas

Relacione cada pregunta con la respuesta apropiada. Tenga en cuenta que hay una respuesta que sobra.

1. How do you do? ( )
2. Are you Ms. Stones? ( )
3. Coffee? ( )
4. Where is she from? ( )
5. Are they Spanish? ( )
6. How old is she? ( )
7. Is he an engineer? ( )

a. Baltimore.
b. Yes, please.
c. Yes, he is.
d. How do you do?
e. No, my name's Green.
f. No, they're Italian.
g. Yes, she is.
h. She's 17.

De persona a persona

2. ¿*a* o *an*?

Bob obtuvo el empleo que buscaba. Después de llegar a casa llamó a su novia Jane para darle la noticia. Complete los espacios en blanco con *a* o *an*.

Jane	Hello?
Bob	Hi, it's Bob.
Jane	Oh, hi Bob.
Bob	Hey, I've got _________ job! I've got _________ new job!
Jane	You've got _________ new job? Where?
Bob	Walker International. It's _________ travel company - _________ international travel company. I'm _________ travel reporter!
Jane	You're not _________ reporter. You're _________ engineer!
Bob	Ah, I'm _________ reporter *now*!
Jane	I see.
Bob	I've got _________ job, and _________ office, and _________ nice boss.
Jane	What's his name?
Bob	Her name is Stones. Her first name is Betty. Betty Stones.
Jane	*Her* name? Your boss is _________ woman? How old is she? Where is she from? Is she single?
Bob	Hey, it's okay! She's married. She has _________ husband and two children.

Palabras mágicas

3. ¿Cuántos años tiene Ud?

Estudie el cuadro de edades y complete las siguientes oraciones.

John is twenty-four. ____________

Jane ____________

María and Peter ____________

Mary ____________

Juan ____________

Alicia ____________

NAME	AGE
John	24
Jane	29
María	32
Peter	32
Mary	59
Juan	62
Alicia	81

4. La familia de Jane

Observe las palabras en el cuadro. Escriba una F al frente de aquellas que sean de género femenino y una M al frente de las que sean de género masculino. A continuación estudie el árbol genealógico de Jane y complete las siguientes oraciones.

- grandfather ____
- grandmother ____
- father ____
- mother ____
- sister ____
- brother ____
- son ____
- daughter ____
- uncle ____
- aunt ____
- niece ____
- nephew ____
- husband ____
- wife ____

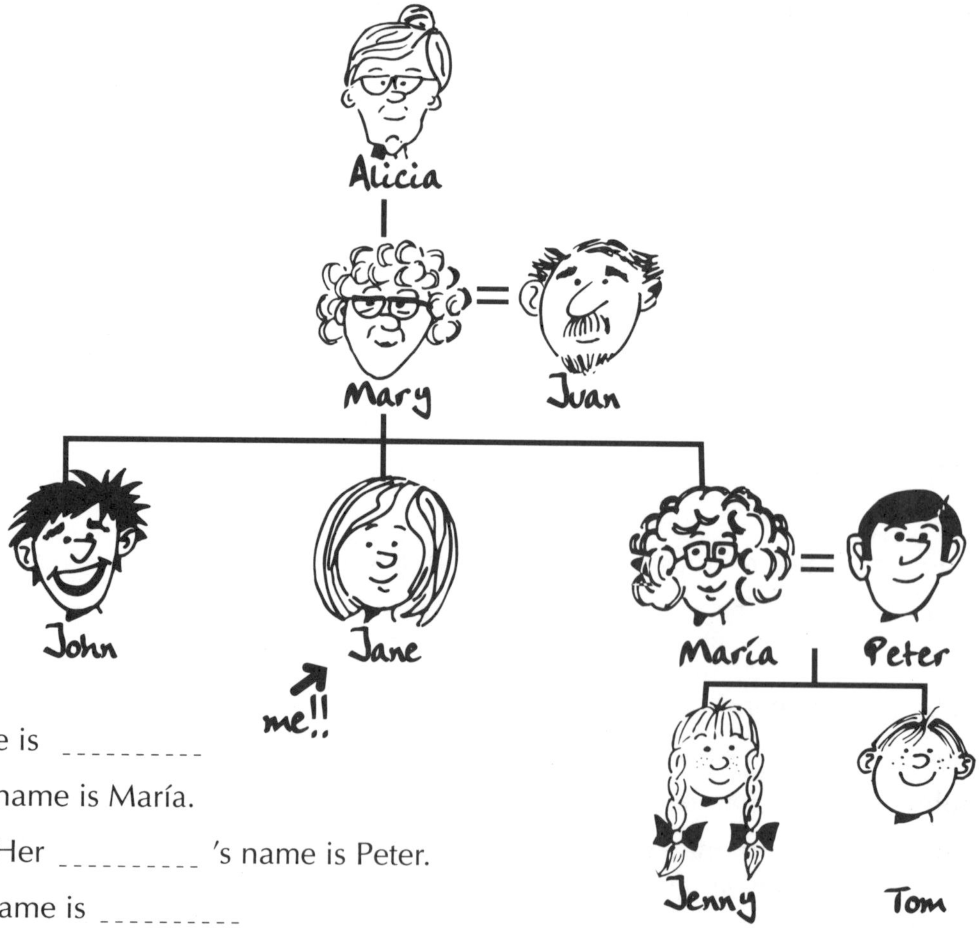

1. My brother's name is __________
2. My __________ 's name is María.
3. María is married. Her __________ 's name is Peter.
4. Their daughter's name is __________
5. Their __________ 's name is Tom.

6. Jenny is my __________ , and Tom is my __________

7. My __________ 's name is Mary, and my __________ 's name is Juan.

8. My __________ 's name is Alicia.

El idioma en la mira

5. *have*

Estudie una vez más el árbol genealógico de Jane y complete estas oraciones.

Ejemplo: María and Peter have two children.

1. John ______________________________ sisters.
2. Jenny ______________________________ brother.
3. Jane ______________________________ niece and one nephew.
4. Mary and Juan ______________________________ children.
5. Jenny and Tom ______________________________ aunts.
6. Alicia ______________________________ grandchildren.

6. Hagamos preguntas

Ordene las palabras de la izquierda para construir preguntas que concuerden con las respuestas de la derecha.

Ejemplo: address/is/Bob's/what **Q** What is Bob's address?

A. It's 28 River Street West, Los Angeles.

1. you/car/do/have/a **Q** ______________________________?

   A. Yes, I have.

2. John/a/does/have/girlfriend **Q** ______________________________?

   A. No, he hasn't.

3. Mr./from/Thomas/where/and/Mrs./are **Q** ______________________________?

   A. From New York.

4. boss's/your/is/what/name **Q** ______________________________?

   A. It's Betty Stones.

5. old/are/children/María's/how **Q** ______________________________?

   A. Four and seven.

6. husband's/is/what/job/her **Q** ______________________________?

   A. He's an accountant.

Texto en contexto

> DEAR MOM AND POP, HOW ARE YOU? I'M FINE.
> GOOD NEWS - I'VE GOT A NEW JOB! I'M NOT AN ENGINEER NOW
> - I'M A REPORTER, A TRAVEL REPORTER. IT'S A BIG COMPANY -
> IT HAS BRANCHES IN LOS ANGELES, NEW YORK, PARIS,
> MADRID, CARACAS - AND TOKYO!! OH, AND ITS NAME IS
> WALKER INTERNATIONAL.
> LOVE, Bob
> P.S. I'VE GOT A NEW GIRLFRIEND, TOO. HER NAME IS JANE, AND
> SHE'S FROM BALTIMORE. SHE'S A PHOTOGRAPHER.

7. Una tarjeta postal

Lea la postal que Bob le mandó a sus padres y corrija los siguientes enunciados, siguiendo el ejemplo.

Ejemplo: Bob has bad news. No, he doesn't. He has good news.

1. Bob has a new car. ____________________
2. Bob is an engineer now. ____________________
3. Walker International is a small company. ____________________
4. It has five branches. ____________________
5. Bob's girlfriend is a reporter. ____________________

¡A escribir!

8. Las preguntas del policía

En su viaje de regreso a casa, Betty es detenida por un policía, que le hace una serie de preguntas.. Complete el diálogo llenando los espacios con las preguntas y las respuestas apropiadas.

Policeman Excuse me.
Betty Yes?
Policeman (Mrs. Betty Jones?) Are you Mrs. Betty Jones?
Betty (no - Betty Stones) No, I'm not. I'm Betty Stones.
Policeman (address 47 Elm Street?) ____________________
Betty (no - 47 Oak Street) ____________________
Policeman (married?) ____________________
Betty (yes) ____________________
Policeman (husband's name?) ____________________
Betty (Phil) ____________________
Policeman (accountant?) ____________________
Betty (no - teacher) ____________________
Policeman (from New York?) ____________________
Betty (no - Chicago) ____________________
Policeman Oh, I see. I'm sorry. I'm very sorry. My mistake! Goodbye!

UNIDAD 3: Where's your office?

En esta unidad aprenderemos a describir la ubicación de los objetos. Hablaremos también de la casa, la oficina y el hotel; las cosas que se encuentran dentro de esos lugares y los colores.

Juegos de palabras

1. ¿Dónde está el gato?

Relacione cada frase con el dibujo apropiado.

1.

2.

3.

4.

5.

6.

7.

a. under the window
b. on the chair
c. in the corner
d. behind the sofa
e. next to the television
f. between the television and the sofa
g. near the door

De persona a persona

2. En la oficina

Bob habla con su madre por teléfono sobre su nuevo trabajo en la compañia Walker International. Complete el siguiente diálogo.

Mother Where is the company, Bob?

Bob It's (in/on) __________ Greenwood. It's the big white building, next to the Fairview Hotel.

Mother Oh, yes. And how many people (is/are) __________ there in Walker International?

Bob (There/They) __________ are fifty-three people in the Greenwood branch.

Mother	(Do/Does) __________ you have an office?	
Bob	Yes, I do. But there are five people in it, so there are five computers, five desks, five chairs and five telephones too - and it's a small office! And it has pink (door/doors) __________ and a pink carpet. But it's nice - there's a big window, and there's a park (behind/next) __________ the building.	
Mother	Are there any women in your office?	
Bob	Yes, there are (one/two) __________ women.	
Mother	And are there any stores (near/next) __________ the office? Or restaurants?	
Bob	Yes, there's an Italian restaurant. And there's a small coffee shop (behind/between) __________ the hotel.	

Palabras mágicas

3. Los colores

Hay once colores escondidos en la sopa de letras.
¿Puede Ud. ubicarlos? Ya hemos encontrado el primero.

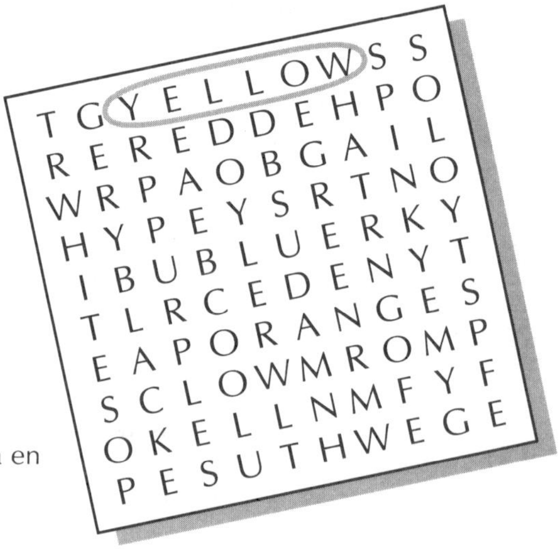

4. Una palabra de más

Encierre en un círculo la palabra que no tiene relación con la palabra en negrilla.

1. **office**: desk shop chair computer telephone boss
2. **living room**: sofa carpet chair toilet television table
3. **kitchen**: lobby refrigerator washing machine knife sink window
4. **bathroom**: sink bath shower soap egg door
5. **house**: bedroom toilet garage yard bathroom gym

El idioma en la mira

5. *a/an/some/any*

Complete los espacios con *a, an, some* o *any*.

1. There are __________ stores and restaurants near the office.
2. My sister has __________ red sports car.
3. Are there __________ hotels in Greenwood?

4. Is there __________ swimming pool in this hotel?
5. There aren't __________ eggs in the refrigerator.
6. There are __________ French and German people in the lobby.
7. Does Bob have __________ brothers and sisters?
8. Is there __________ orange umbrella under the table?

6. Hagamos preguntas

Utilizando las siguientes palabras construya preguntas y dé respuestas cortas.

Ejemplo: sofa/living room — Is there a sofa in the living room?
Yes, there is

1. shower/bathroom ______________________
Yes,

2. washing machine/kitchen ______________________
No,

3. eggs/refrigerator ______________________
Yes,

4. restaurants/Greenwood ______________________
Yes,

5. women/your office ______________________
No,

6. pink carpet/living room ______________________
Yes,

Texto en contexto

7. En el hotel Fairview

Lea la descripción de la distribución del primer piso del hotel Fairview y escriba en el plano el nombre de los diversos cuartos que aparecen en él.

There is a large French restaurant next to the lobby on the left, and there's a small coffee shop next to the lobby on the right. There's a bookstore between the coffee shop and the travel office. The public telephones are near the travel office. There's a small gym next to the sauna, and a small swimming pool behind the gym. There are restrooms in the corner near the restaurant. In the corner of the lobby there are some sofas, chairs and coffee tables.

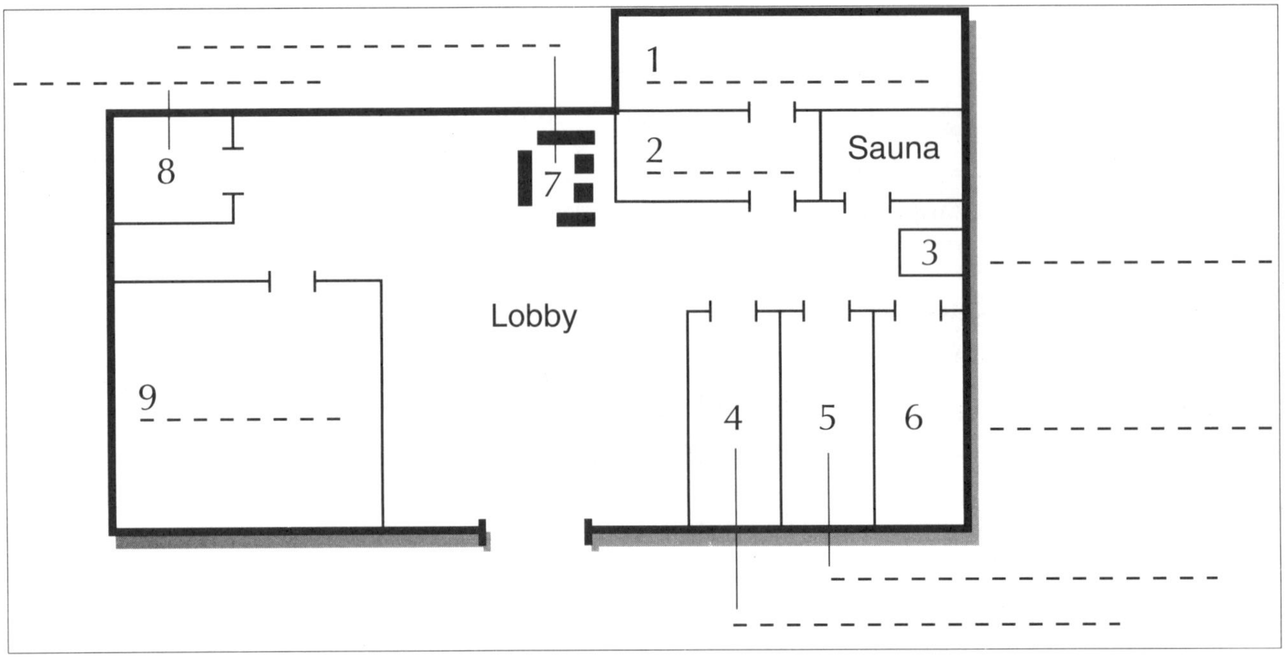

¡A escribir!

8. La nueva casa de Jane

Jane, la novia de Bob, se mudó recientemente a una casa nueva. Estudie la información que aparece a continuación y escriba preguntas que concuerden con las siguientes respuestas.

Ejemplo: Is there a shower? ____________

No, there isn't.

1. ____________

   There are two.

2. ____________

   Yes, there is. It's in the kitchen.

3. ____________

   It's yellow.

4. ____________

   It's next to the house.

5 ____________

   Yes, there are three apple trees.

6. ____________

   It's behind the house.

UNIDAD 4: Do you love me?

En la unidad 4 se haremos ejercicios sobre la hora, los deportes y los pasatiempos. También hablaremos sobre gastos y preferencias.

Juegos de palabras

1. Palabras que riman

Una con una flecha las palabras que terminan en sonidos parecidos..

De persona a persona

2. La hora del desayuno

Betty Stones acaba de preparar el desayuno y está esperando que sus hijos Linda y Andy y su esposo Phil bajen al comedor. Lea la conversación y conteste las preguntas que aparecen en la página siguiente.

Betty Breakfast! Breakfast time! Where are they? Where are the children? Breakfast is ready!

Phil Breakfast is ready, but the children aren't. Linda is still in the bath, and Andy is still in bed. And he has my newspaper.

Betty What?! But it's 8:00 (eight o'clock) ! It's late. Breakfast is on the table.

Phil I'm ready. Ham and eggs - good. I love ham and eggs. Ah, here's Linda.

Linda Morning, Mom, morning, Pop.

Betty You're late - it's 8:00. And now I'm late, and your father's late too.

Linda Sorry. Is this my breakfast? Ham and eggs? Oh, yuk! No, thank you.

Betty What? But you like ham and eggs!

Linda No, I don't. I don't like meat. I hate meat! I'm a vegetarian.

Betty You? You're not a vegetarian.

Linda Yes, I am. I'm a vegetarian now. Is there any coffee?

Ejemplo: Who's in the bath? Linda is in the bath.

1. Who's still in bed? ______
2. Who has Phil's newspaper? ______
3. Who's ready? ______
4. Who likes ham and eggs? ______
5. Who doesn't like meat? ______
6. Who's a vegetarian? ______

Palabras mágicas

3. ¿Qué hora es?

Observe los relojes y escriba la hora correcta debajo de cada uno.

Ejemplo:

1. ______
2. ______

It's half past nine

3. ______
4. ______

4. ¿Dónde está Bob a las siete?

Construya oraciones sobre la rutina diaria de Bob utilizando las frases que aparecen en el cuadro.

Ejemplo: 7:00 At seven o'clock he's in bed.

1. 7:30 ______
2. 8:30 ______
3. 9:00 ______
4. 1:00 ______
5. 6:30 ______
6. 8:30 ______

the coffee shop
in the bath
in the bar
in bed
in his car
in his office
in the gym

5. ¿Qué te gusta más?

Ordene las siguientes oraciones, comenzando con la que expresa un mayor grado de preferencia.

1. I like it a bit. I love it.
2. I hate it. ______________________
3. I like it very much. ______________________
4. I don't like it very much. ______________________
5. It's okay. ______________________
6. I love it. ______________________
7. I don't like it at all. ______________________

El idioma en la mira

6. ¿Me quieres?

Escoja la palabra apropiada para llenar cada espacio en blanco.

me you him her it them us

1. I don't like my job at all. In fact, I hate __________
2. Do you like cats? Yes, I love __________
3. My boss's name is Betty Stones - I like __________
4. I like Uncle John, but my husband doesn't like __________ at all
5. I love Pete, but he doesn't love __________
6. Where's my umbrella? Betty, do you have __________ ?
7. We don't like our new teacher, and she doesn't like __________ !
8. A new sports car!! Thank you, Pop. I love __________ !

7. Respuestas cortas

Formule respuestas cortas a estas preguntas como en el ejemplo.

Ejemplo: Is it 10:00? Yes, it is.

1. Is Linda still in the bath? Yes, ______________________
2. Does your daughter like her new teacher? No, ______________________
3. Sorry, Mom - am I late? No, ______________________
4. Do you like red wine? Yes, ______________________
5. Are you a vegetarian? Yes, ______________________
6. Do they like Detroit? No, ______________________

Texto en contexto

8. Le gusta el vino tinto pero...

Bob ha identificado contrastes entre sus gustos y los de su novia Jane Estudie los siguientes apartes de una carta que él ha enviado a un amigo y escriba de nuevo las frases en el orden correcto.

a. meat, but she's a vegetarian. She

b. like it very much. She likes swimming and

c. She likes red wine, but

d. loves shopping, but I hate it. I

e. I like beer. I love

f. like dancing, but she doesn't

g. like her? Yes, I do.

h. golf, but I don't. Do I

¡A escribir!

9. ¿Le gusta bailar?

Betty Stones va a reunirse con sus amigos Pete y Jenny el sábado. Están decidiendo qué van a hacer, porque cada uno tiene gustos diferentes. Construya preguntas y respuestas sobre las cosas que les gustan.

	Pete	**Betty**	**Jenny**	**you**
golf	very much!	not very much	not at all	?
shopping	hate it	not really	love it!	?
dancing	it's okay	Yuk!!! hate it	no!!! hate it	?
bars	love them	like them	not really	?

Ejemplo: Pete/golf Q. Does Pete like golf?
A. Yes, he does. He likes it very much.

1. Jenny/shopping? Q. ________________ A. ________________
2. Betty and Jenny/dancing? Q. ________________ A. ________________
3. Jenny/golf? Q. ________________ A. ________________
4. Pete/bars? Q. ________________ A. ________________
5. you/golf? shopping? dancing? bars? Q. ________________ A. ________________

UNIDAD 5: Are you free tomorrow?

En esta unidad hablaremos sobre la rutina diaria y sobre la frecuencia con que realizamos ciertas actividades. También haremos ejercicios sobre la hora y los días de la semana.

Juegos de palabras

1. ¿Qué hora es?

Relacione cada reloj con la hora correcta.

1. quarter past seven
2. quarter past three
3. four fifteen
4. quarter to four
5. nine forty-five
6. eight fifteen
7. quarter to twelve
8. quarter to one

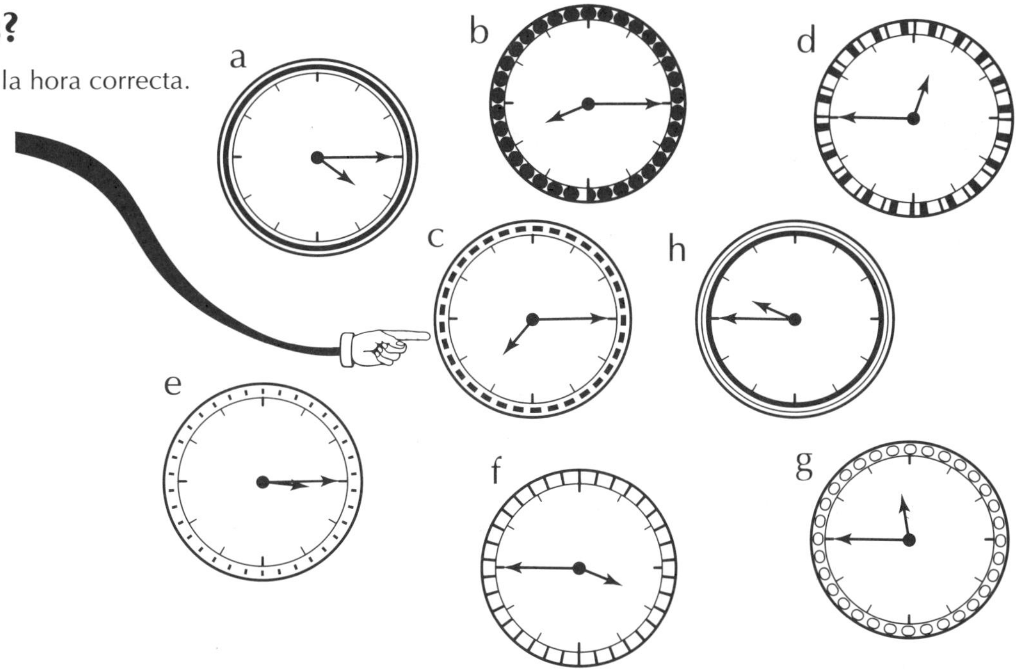

De persona a persona

2. ¿Salimos juntos?

Esta es la segunda semana de trabajo de Bob. Al llegar el lunes por la mañana, sostiene una breve conversación con Anne, la recepcionista. Complete los espacios en blanco con el verbo apropiado del cuadro.

eat watch meet(x2) play(x2) learn(x2) cook visit read

Anne Morning, Bob.

Bob Morning, Anne. Ummm... Anne? Are you busy this evening? I'm free, so...

Anne Sorry, Bob. I _________ tennis on Mondays. I always _________ tennis on Mondays.

Bob I see. How about tomorrow? Are you free tomorrow evening?

Anne That's Tuesday. No, I'm sorry, but I _________ Spanish on Tuesdays. And I _________ the guitar on Wednesdays.

Bob Hmmm. This is difficult. What do you do on Thursdays and Fridays? Do you __________ Japanese poetry? Do you __________ Chinese food?

Anne No, I don't. I usually __________ TV at home on Thursdays, and I always __________ my parents on Fridays, and __________ dinner at their house.

Bob And the weekend? How about Saturday and Sunday?

Anne I never __________ strange men on the weekend.

Bob I'm not strange! I'm Bob!

Anne Sorry, but I always __________ my boyfriend on the weekend. And you've got a girlfriend, Bob.

Palabras mágicas

3. Encuentre el verbo

Escriba el verbo más apropiado para cada dibujo.

Ejemplo

drink

a. __________

b. __________

c. __________

d. __________

e. __________

f. __________

4. Rutina diaria

Enumere del uno al once estas actividades, de acuerdo con el orden en que Ud. suele realizarlas y marque en el reloj la hora en que las hace.

______ read the newspaper
______ eat breakfast
______ cook dinner

______ go to bed
______ take a shower/bath
______ start work
______ get up
______ finish work
______ watch TV
______ go to work
______ have lunch

El idioma en la mira

5. Oraciones en desorden

Ordene las siguientes palabras para hacer oraciones.

1. football always Saturdays I on play

   ----

2. parents visits Anne her often

   ----

3. Bob his work to usually car drives

   ----

4. red often drink don't wine I

   ----

5. Fridays Betty gym to sometimes goes the on

   ----

6. meat eats Linda never

   ----

6. Hagamos preguntas

Complete las oraciones con *do* o *does,* y utilice respuestas cortas siguiendo el ejemplo.

Ejemplo: Does she always get up at 7:15? Yes, she does.

1. __________ the children like their new school? Yes, __________ .
2. __________ he work in Miami? No, __________ .
3. __________ you often write letters? No, __________ .
4. __________ your parents live in Washington? Yes, __________ .
5. __________ your sister eat meat? No, __________ .
6. __________ you drive a car? Yes, __________ .

Texto en contexto

7. El diario de Jane

Jane, la novia de Bob, piensa que su vida es aburrida y que necesita un cambio. Lea esta página de su diario y llene los espacios en blanco con *to, at, on* o *in*.

¡A escribir!

8. Hablemos de Ud.

Conteste las siguientes preguntas con información sobre Ud. mismo.

1. Where do you live? --
2. Do you often play tennis? --
3. What time do you usually get up? --
4. What time do you usually have lunch? --
5. What do you usually do on Sunday? --
6. Do you drive a car? --

UNIDAD 6: How much is this?

Esta unidad trata sobre las compras. Practicaremos la formulación de preguntas acerca de algunos artículos, precios y dinero.

Juegos de palabras

1. Conversación en la tienda

Relacione el principio y el final de estas oraciones, colocando el número apropiado en cada paréntesis.

1. This skirt	( )	a. like the color.
2. Can I	( )	b. this in size 12?
3. I want a	( )	c. is nice.
4. How much is	( )	d. blue sweater.
5. I don't	( )	e. jeans.
6. What size	( )	f. help you?
7. Do you have	( )	g. do you wear?
8. I like these	( )	h. this watch?

De persona a persona

2. El regalo de cumpleaños de Bob

Pronto será el cumpleaños de Bob, y Jane ha ido a comprarle un regalo, con su amiga Pat. Lea la conversación y responda a las siguientes preguntas.

Pat This shirt is nice.

Jane Yes, it is, but Bob doesn't like brown.

Pat What colors does he usually wear?

Jane He likes blue or gray or black. Sometimes he wears green.

Pat How about this one? It's a nice color.

Jane What size is it? Medium. How much is it? Where's the label?

Pat Here it is. What!? $99.00 (ninety-nine dollars)!?

Jane It's silk. I don't like that price at all.

Clerk Good morning. Can I help you?

Jane Yes, please. I want a cotton shirt, in blue or gray. A casual shirt. It's for my boyfriend.

Clerk What size does he wear?

Jane I don't know. Medium, maybe.

Clerk These shirts are very popular now. Or these?

Jane They're nice. How much are they?

Clerk They're $55.00.

Jane What? $55.00? I don't have $55.00!

Pat How about a tie? These are cheap.

Jane Good idea. I don't want an expensive present. I don't like Bob very much now. A cheap tie is a good idea.

1. What colors does Bob like? ______________________
2. Does he like brown? ______________________
3. How much is the silk shirt? ______________________
4. Does Jane want a cotton shirt or a silk shirt? ______________________
5. Does she have $55.00? ______________________
6. Does she know Bob's size? ______________________

P

Palabras mágicas

3. Descubra la ropa

Ordene las letras y descubra las palabras relacionadas con la ropa.

Ejemplo: resed ___dress___

1. trish	______________	6. janes	______________
2. trawees	______________	7. hoses	______________
3. cossk	______________	8. catkej	______________
4. trisk	______________	9. sluboe	______________
5. ite	______________	10. toca	______________

4. Dinero, dinero, dinero

Escriba estos precios en palabras.

Ejemplo: $3.50 ___three (dollars) fifty (cents)___

1. $7.00 ______________________
2. $1.45 ______________________
3. $4.99 ______________________
4. $6.50 ______________________

5. $15.00 ____________________

6. $49.99 ____________________

7. $125.00 ____________________

8. $500.00 ____________________

El idioma en la mira

5. *do, don't, does, doesn't...*

Llene los espacios con *do/don't, does/doesn't,is/isn't* o *are/aren't* según corresponda.

1. Excuse me, how much __________ these gloves?
2. __________ you have this skirt in green?
3. What color __________ you want?
4. I'm sorry, I __________ want a medium, I want a large.
5. __________ this silk or cotton?
6. What size __________ he take?
7. This bag __________ nice - how much is it?
8. These shoes __________ my size - they're size 6. Do you have size 7?

6. ¿Cuánto cuesta?

Haga preguntas sobre los precios de estos artículos y contéstelas.

Ejemplo:

Q: How much are these gloves?
A: They're five (dollars) ninety-nine.

$5.99

1. $35.00

2. $9.50

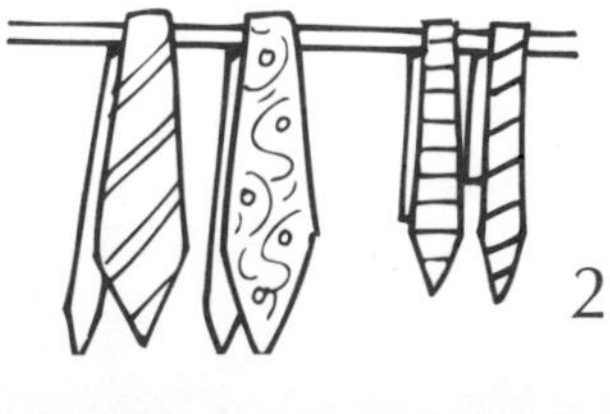

3. $24.99

4. 50¢

5. $7.50

6. $2.50

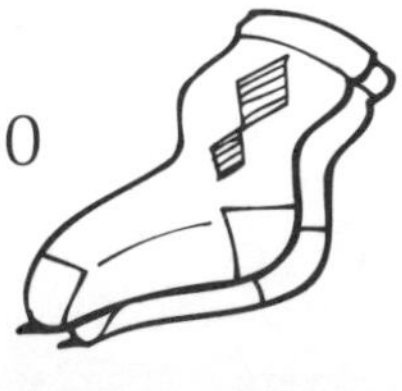

Texto en contexto

7. ¿Quién hace la comida?

Lea la descripción siguiente y llene los espacios con la forma correcta de los verbos de la izquierda.

hate
eat (x2)
go (x2)
buy
like (x3)
come
cook (x2)

Betty __________ shopping, but she __________ cooking. Her husband, Phil, __________ cooking, but doesn't __________ shopping very much. So Betty usually __________ to the supermarket after work, and __________ food for dinner. Then Phil __________ home at about 6:30, and __________ dinner. (This is sometimes difficult - their daughter Linda doesn't __________ meat, and their son Andy doesn't __________ fish.) On the weekend, sometimes the children __________ , and sometimes they all __________ to a restaurant for dinner. This is expensive - but it's easy.

¡Al escribir!

8. De compras

Haga preguntas que concuerden con estas respuestas.

Ejemplo: Do you have any silk shirts?

No, I'm sorry. We don't have any silk shirts.

1. ______________________________

She takes a size 12.

2. ______________________________

It's $35.00.

3. ______________________________

It's black and gray.

4. ______________________________

They're 25 cents ($0.25).

5. ______________________________

Yes, please. Do you have any cotton socks?

6. ______________________________

The ties? They're next to the shirts.

UNIDAD 7: The bar's that way.

En la unidad 7 hablaremos sobre las tiendas y los edificios públicos y daremos direcciones. También averigüaremos los horarios de apertura de las tiendas.

Juegos de palabras

1. Está a la izquierda

Una con una línea las descripciones con los dibujos apropiados.

1. opposite
2. third house on the right
3. straight ahead
4. on the left
5. straight on at the intersection
6. on the right
7. second house on the left
8. at the end

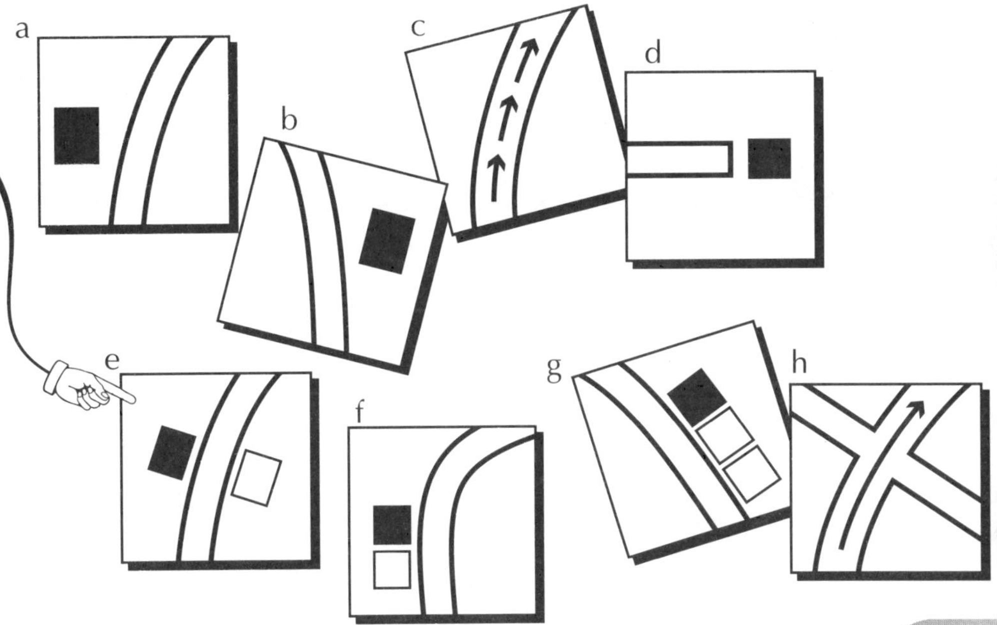

De persona a persona

2. ¿Dónde está la galería?

Bob va en camino para encontrarse con su novia Jane pero está retrasado. Al caminar apresuradamente por la calle lo detiene una joven turista japonesa. Complete el diálogo con la palabra apropiada.

Tourist Excuse me…

Bob Yes, can I help you?

Tourist Is the Victoria Art Gallery (far/near) __________ here?

Bob It's not far. Do you (know/see) __________ the post office on that corner? Turn left (here/there) __________ - that's Baker Street. Go (under/over) __________ the river bridge, and then go straight on Baker Street until you come to a big church (on/at) __________ your right. Turn right there, and the Victoria Art Gallery is on (your/my) __________ left. There's a big sign (inside/outside) __________ . You can't miss it.

Tourist I'm sorry... Do I turn left (or/and) __________ right at the post office? And where is the river bridge? I'm sorry, I don't understand.

Bob Okay, come with (I/me) __________. (Bob goes with her.) Here is the post office. Turn left here. Now, here is the river bridge. By the way, (where/here) __________ are you from?

Tourist I'm from Japan. (She sees Jane across the road.) Excuse me, that woman... is she your friend?

Jane Hey!

Bob Jane! It's Jane, my girlfriend. Er, um, hello!

Jane Hello, Bob. And (who/what) __________ is this? Your new girlfriend? The bar isn't this way - it's that way.

Bob I know, I know, but...

Jane Okay, you go that way - with your new friend. Goodbye!

Palabras mágicas

3. Los números

Llene el cuadro con el número ordinal (*first, second* etc.) que convenga.

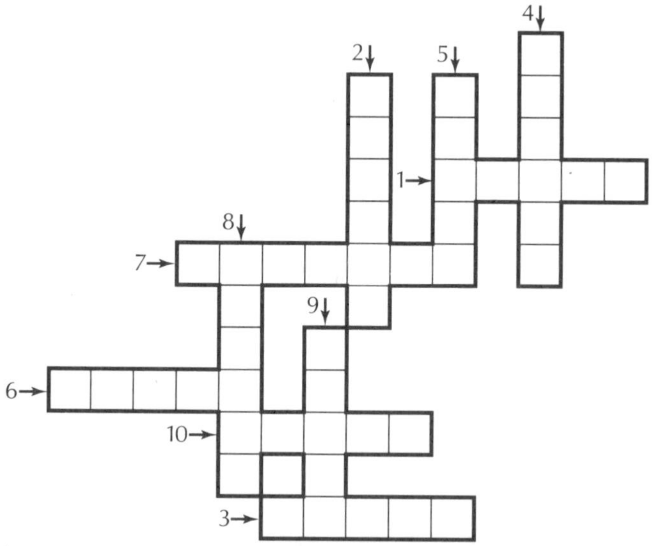

4. En la calle

Elija una de las palabras del cuadro para completar las oraciones.

post office bank
supermarket
butcher's
library bar
restaurant
swimming pool

1. You borrow books from a ______________________________
2. You buy stamps at a ______________________________
3. You swim in a ______________________________
4. You borrow money from a ______________________________
5. You buy food at a ______________________________
6. You buy meat at a ______________________________
7. You eat a meal at a ______________________________
8. You have a drink at a ______________________________

El idioma en la mira

5. ¿*to, at* o *on*?

Complete los espacios con *to, at,* o *on,*según corresponda.

1. The children's department is __________ the third floor.
2. Go straight __________ , until you come to a telephone booth.
3. Turn left __________ the church.
4. Our house is second __________ the right.
5. Which floor is Bob's office __________ ?
6. The swimming pool closes __________ 5:30 __________ Sundays.
7. The post office is __________ Broad Street.
8. Our house is __________ the end of the street.

6. Palabras en desorden

Escriba estas palabras en el orden correcto y forme oraciones.

1. me is there telephone excuse here a booth near

____?

2. on fourth clothes are men's floor the

____

3. closes Sundays the past ten half bar on at

____

4. right big turn by the hotel

____

5. is from o'clock library the open nine weekdays on

____

6. isn't from house far my here

____

Texto en contexto

7. ¿Dónde está la fiesta?

Betty Stones ha invitado a varias personas de la compañia Walker International a una fiesta en su casa. Lea las instrucciones sobre cómo llegar a su casa y marque la ruta en el mapa.

Turn left at the intersection, and go along the road to Whitecross. Take the second right into Forest Drive. Go straight ahead, over the river bridge, until you come to a telephone booth on the left. Take a left here, and our house is the second on the right.

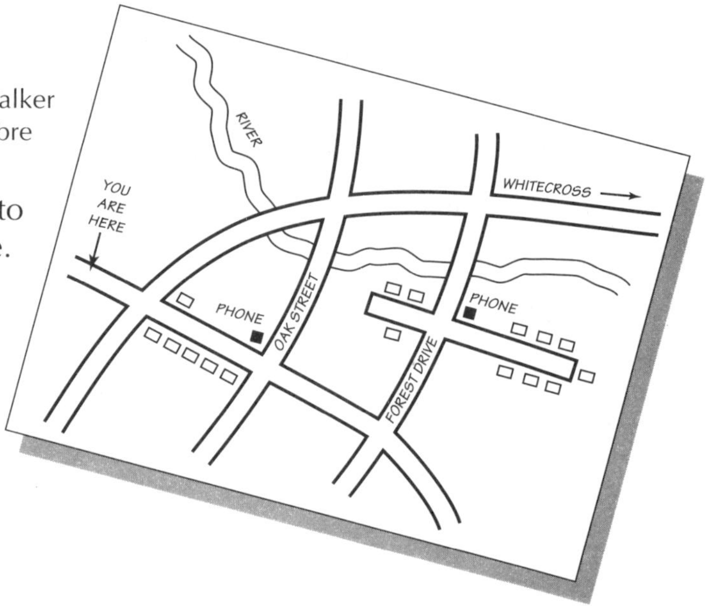

¡A escribir!

8. ¿A qué hora abren?

Observe los horarios de apertura de varios lugares. Haga preguntas y contéstelas, como en el ejemplo.

Ejemplo:

Q. When is the pool open?

A. It's open from nine o'clock to seven o'clock on weekdays, and from ten o'clock to half past five on Sundays. It's closed on Mondays.

1. **Q:** ______________________________

   A: ______________________________

   ____

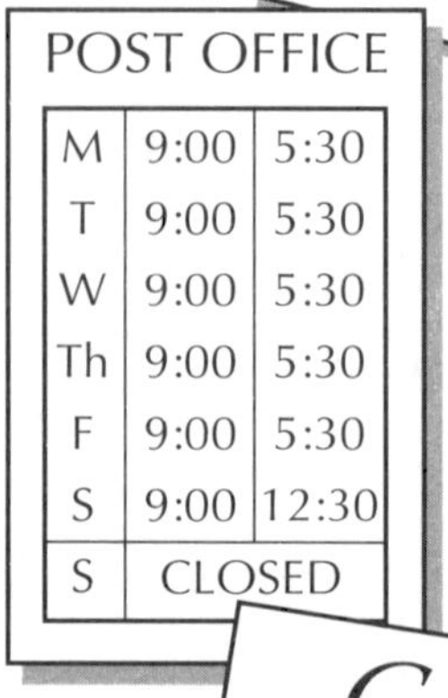

2. **Q:** ______________________________

   A: ______________________________

   ____

3. **Q:** ______________________________

   A: ______________________________

   ____

UNIDAD 8: How was your weekend?

En esta unidad practicaremos conversaciones sobre eventos pasados y sobre las actividades del fin de semana. También haremos preguntas con *what? where? when?* y *who?*.

Juegos de palabras

1. Verbos

Relacione los verbos de la izquierda con las palabras o frases de la derecha.

1. had	( )	a. the way
2. met	( )	b. a drink
3. asked	( )	c. left
4. was	( )	d. home
5. went	( )	e. a friend
6. borrowed	( )	f. tennis
7. turned	( )	g. very nice
8. play	( )	h. a book

De persona a persona

2. ¿Cómo te fue el fin de semana?

El lunes por la mañana, Bob habla con Anne, la recepcionista, sobre su fin de semana. Llene los espacios con la forma correcta del verbo entre paréntesis.

Anne How (be) was your weekend, Bob?

Bob Not good, not good at all.

Anne Why? What (happen) _________ ?

Bob Jane and I (have) _________ an argument on Saturday.

Anne Oh, I see. Why did you (have) _________ an argument?

Bob She (see) _________ me with another woman.

Anne Bob!

Bob But she (be) _________ only a tourist! She (ask) _________ me the way to Victoria Art Gallery, and I (tell) _________ her the way. She didn't (understand) _________ English very well, so I (go) _________ to the art gallery with her. She (be) _________ Japanese. She (be) _________ very nice.

Anne But you (have) _________ a date with Jane on Saturday.

Bob I know. That (be) _________ the problem. I (be) _________ late for the date. And then Jane (see) _________ us in Bridge Street.

Palabras mágicas

3. Sobra una

¿Cuál es la palabra que sobra en cada renglón?

1. tennis swimming gym golf jogging
2. bridge restaurant bar supermarket library
3. went ate played met go
4. morning tomorrow afternoon evening night
5. where when white what who

4. ¿Cuál es la palabra adecuada?

Escoja una palabra de cada uno de los grupos mencionados arriba para completar las oraciones.

1. Did you go to the pool yesterday?
   No, I don't really like __________.
2. I wanted some stamps, so I went to the __________.
3. I __________ Phil at the gym yesterday.
4. We all got up at 7:00 this __________.
5. __________ did she buy?

El idioma en la mira

5. Plurales

Escriba los plurales de las palabras que aparacen en la tabla.

Singular	Plural
I	we
child	
man	
library	
church	

Singular	Plural
shoe	
woman	
family	
this	
person	

6. *was* o *were*?

Llene los espacios con *was* o *were*, según corresponda.

1. These shoes _______ very expensive.
2. Her boss's name _______ John Brooks.
3. How _______ your weekend?
4. Where _______ Bob and Jane yesterday?
5. My son _______ ten on Tuesday.
6. Who _______ in the bar yesterday?

7. Preguntas

Haga preguntas adecuadas a las respuestas, siguiendo el ejemplo.

Ejemplo: What time did you go to the bar?
We went to the bar at 7:30.

1. Where ______________________________?
   I went to Bellevue yesterday.
2. When ______________________________?
   I met her on Sunday.
3. What ______________________________ at the restaurant?
   He ate fish.
4. How many ______________________________ from the library?
   I borrowed three books.
5. Where ______________________________ shopping?
   They went shopping in Vancouver.
6. What time ______________________________ on Sunday?
   She got up at 10:00.

Texto en contexto

8. El diario de Jane

Jane siempre escribe su diario antes de dormirse. Lea la siguiente sección y conteste las preguntas que aparecen a continuación.

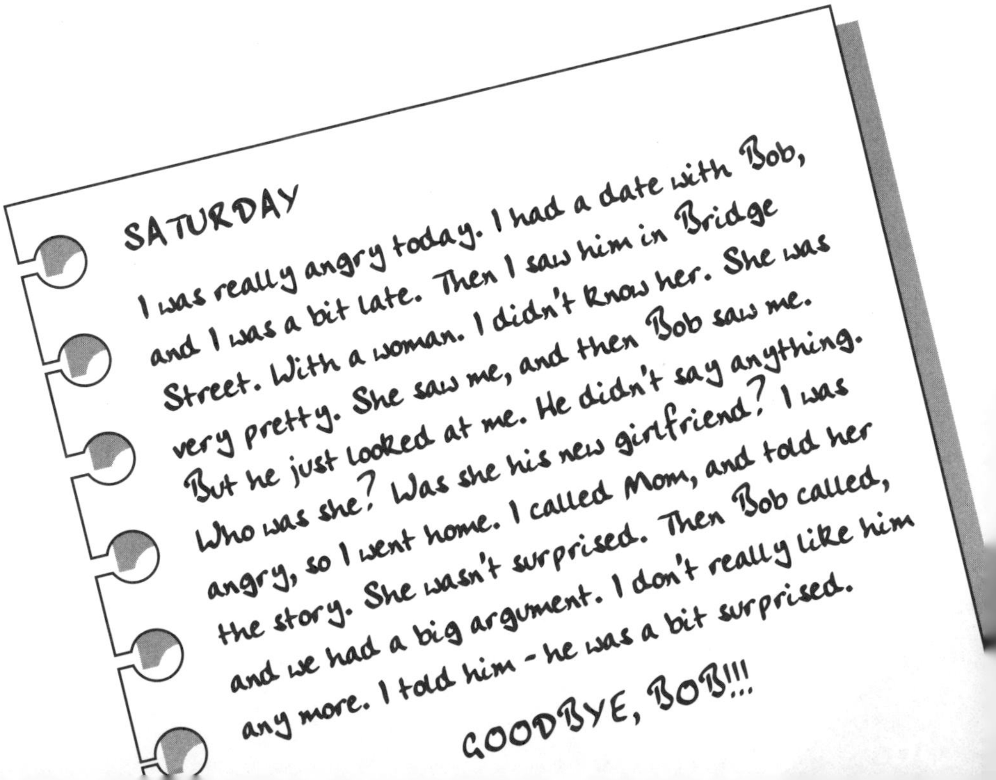
SATURDAY

I was really angry today. I had a date with Bob, and I was a bit late. Then I saw him in Bridge Street. With a woman. I didn't know her. She was very pretty. She saw me, and then Bob saw me. But he just looked at me. He didn't say anything. Who was she? Was she his new girlfriend? I was angry, so I went home. I called Mom, and told her the story. She wasn't surprised. Then Bob called, and we had a big argument. I don't really like him any more. I told him - he was a bit surprised.

GOODBYE, BOB!!!

Ejemplo: Who did Jane have a date with? *She had a date with Bob.*

1. Where did Jane see Bob? ____________________
2. Who was he with? ____________________
3. Did Bob and the woman see Jane? ____________________
4. Where did Jane go? ____________________
5. Who did Jane call? ____________________
6. Who called Jane? ____________________

¡A escribir!

9. ¿Qué hicieron el fin de semana?

Estas personas apuntaron las citas que tenían para el fin de semana. Haga preguntas sobre lo que hizo cada una de ellas y contéstelas, como en el ejemplo.

Ejemplo:

Betty

Q: What did Betty do on Sunday morning?
A: She played tennis.

1.Jane

2. Bob

3. Phil

4. Ana

5. María

1. **Q:** ____________________
   A: ____________________
2. **Q:** ____________________
   A: ____________________
3. **Q:** ____________________
   A: ____________________
4. **Q:** ____________________
   A: ____________________
5. **Q:** ____________________
   A: ____________________

UNIDAD 9: We went camping.

En la unidad 9 encontraremos nuevos ejercicios sobre el pasado. También describiremos sus vacaciones, medios de transporte y la fecha.

Juegos de palabras

1. Respuestas cortas

Escriba el número de la pregunta apropiada para cada respuesta.

1. Did you like Mexico?
2. Is it hot in Spain in summer?
3. Did your sister go camping last year?
4. Did your parents travel by train?
5. Do you always go skiing in winter?
6. Did you go with your boyfriend?
7. Was your hotel near the sea?
8. Does she like skiing?

( ) a. No, she didn't.
( ) b. No, they didn't.
( ) c. Yes, she does.
( ) d. Yes, we did.
( ) e. No, it wasn't.
( ) f. Yes, we do.
( ) g. Yes, it is.
( ) h. Yes, I did.

De persona a persona

2. ¿Hotel o tienda de campaña?

Bob está en el bar esperando a su amigo Ray para tomar una copa. Mientras espera estudia algunos folletos turísticos para planear sus vacaciones. Llene los espacios del diálogo con la forma correcta del verbo.

Ray What are those? Travel brochures?

Bob Yes, for my summer vacation. Last year I (go) __________ to Florida, and I really (enjoy) __________ it.

Ray Where (stay) __________ ? In a hotel?

Bob Yes, it (be) __________ a big hotel, near the beach, with a pool, and a really good restaurant, and disco every night.

Ray I (hate) __________ those big hotels!

Bob Really? Why? It (be) __________ good fun - I (eat) __________ a lot of good food, I (drink __________ a lot of good wine and beer, I (swim) __________ , I (dance) __________ , and I (meet) __________ a lot of very attractive women! Where did *you* go last year?

Ray	I didn't have a lot of money last year, so I (go) __________ camping with some friends. We (have) __________ a great time.
Bob	Camping? Yuk! Wasn't it cold and wet?
Ray	No, it (be) __________ ! The weather (be) __________ good, and we (go) __________ hiking, and swimming, and sightseeing.
Bob	(cook) __________ ?
Ray	Sometimes we (cook) __________ , and sometimes we (eat) __________ out - in bars, or cheap restaurants. And we (meet) __________ a lot of attractive women, too.
Bob	I don't believe you!

Palabras mágicas

3. ¡El tiempo pasa!

Escriba los años en palabras, siguiendo el ejemplo.

Ejemplo: 1979 nineteen seventy-nine

1. 1985 ______________________
2. 1960 ______________________
3. 1881 ______________________
4. 1994 ______________________
5. 1700 ______________________
6. 1979 ______________________
7. 1990 ______________________
8. 1912 ______________________

4. ¿Cómo viajaste?

Ordene estas palabras y descubra diferentes modos de viajar.

Ejemplo: ubs bus

1. liccbey ______________________
2. inart ______________________
3. arc ______________________
4. nepal ______________________
5. axit ______________________
6. troocmecly ______________________
7. yaswub ______________________
8. roshe ______________________

El idioma en la mira

5. Verbos en pasado

Complete las listas de los cuadros llenando los espacios con el presente o el pasado de los verbos.

Presente	Pasado
go	went
eat	
swim	
drink	
enjoy	
like	
stay	
want	

Presente	Pasado
have	had
	saw
	told
	danced
	met
	traveled
	drove
	did

6. Formas negativas

Exprese su desacuerdo respecto a estas afirmaciones, como en el ejemplo.

Ejemplo: They went hiking. (skiing) No, they didn't go hiking, they went skiing.

1. She swam in the sea. (pool) ______________________________
2. They went walking every night. (jogging) ______________________________
3. Betty and her family stayed in a hotel. (tent) ______________________________
4. We went to Costa Rica in 1989. (1988) ______________________________
5. They traveled by car. (train) ______________________________
6. He checked the oil in the car. (water) ______________________________

Texto en contexto

7. Todo acerca de Betty Stones

Lea la información acerca de Betty Stones y haga preguntas que concuerden con las siguientes respuestas.

Betty Stones was born in Ireland in 1944. Her mother was a teacher and her father was an engineer. The family came to the United States in 1954 - Betty was ten. They lived in Chicago.

Betty went to college in Boston and studied economics. She was a good student, and she enjoyed college. She also enjoyed traveling, and went to Europe and India by bus and train.

After college, she moved to Los Angeles, and she met her husband Phil there. They got married in 1969.

1. ______________________ In nineteen forty-four.
2. ______________________ In nineteen fifty-four.
3. ______________________ In Chicago.
4. ______________________ In Boston.
5. ______________________ Economics
6. ______________________ In nineteen sixty-nine.

¡A escribir!

8. Consultando la lista

Betty y su familia van a ir a acampar este fin de semana. Betty preparó una lista de cosas que tiene que hacer hoy. Haga preguntas y respuestas sobre lo que ella hizo y sobre lo que no pudo hacer.

Ejemplo: *check oil and water in car* ✓

Did she check the oil and water in the car? Yes, she did.

1. *call camp site* ✓ ______________________
2. *buy food* ✓ ______________________
3. *clean car* ✗ ______________________
4. *go to bank* ✗ ______________________
5. *clean hiking boots* ✓ ______________________
6. *check tent* ✓ ______________________

UNIDAD 10: Are you hungry?

En la unidad 10 hablaremos sobre las comidas en los restaurantes. Podremos practicar cómo ordenar comida en un restaurante, cómo comprar los alimentos y cómo expresar el peso y las medidas de los productos.

Juegos de palabras

1. En el restaurante

Relacione la pregunta con la respuesta apropiada.

1. Would you like anything to drink?	( )	a. White, please.
2. Salad or vegetables?	( )	b. No, tea, please.
3. Do you want some coffee?	( )	c. Yes, I'd like a ham salad, please.
4. Red or white wine?	( )	d. No, I'm a vegetarian.
5. Are you ready to order?	( )	e. Salad.
6. Are you hungry?	( )	f. Yes, some red wine, please.
7. Do you like meat?	( )	g. Yes, I am.

De persona a persona

2. ¿Qué desea?

Jane sigue enojada con Bob, pero después de dos días él la invita a comer para conversar.

1. **Jane** Yes, okay, a chicken sandwich. And some coffee.
2. **Jane** I had their tomato soup last week, and it was horrible.
3. **Jane** I don't know. I'm not really hungry.
4. **Jane** And I'd like a chicken sandwich.
5. **Bob** French fries, please.
6. **Bob** Oh. Well, how about a sandwich?
7. **Bob** Yes, I'd like a cheese omelet, please.
8. **Bob** How about some soup? The tomato soup is good here.
9. **Bob** What do you want?

10. **Bob** Yes, one coffee and one orange juice, please.

11. **Waiter** With a salad, or with french fries?

12. **Waiter** Are you ready to order?

13. **Waiter** One cheese omelet and french fries, and one chicken sandwich. Would you like anything to drink?

Bob What do you want? --

Jane --

Bob --

Jane --

Bob --

Jane --

Waiter --

------ --

------ --

------ --

------ --

------ --

------ --

Palabras mágicas

3. ¿Fruta, verduras o carnes?

Agrupe las siguientes palabras en la categoría apropiada:

chicken, lettuce, apple, lamb, banana, pear, beef, potato, ham, peas, lemon, beans, carrots, pork, onion, sausages, orange, steak, strawberry

FRUIT	VEGETABLES	MEAT

4. Lista de compras

Estudie la lista de compras y escriba los artículos y las cantidades en forma completa.

Ejemplo: 3 lbs potatoes ______ three pounds of potatoes ______

1/2 lb tomatoes	1.	__________	1 lt milk	4.	__________
2 pts beer	2.	__________	8 oz ham	5.	__________
1 kg apples	3.	__________	1 gal oil	6.	__________

El idioma en la mira

5. ¿Se pueden contar?

Escriba *a, an* antes de los artículos que generalmente se pueden contar, y *some* delante de aquellos que no se cuentan.

1. __________ red wine	5. __________ soup	9. __________ sausage
2. __________ glass of wine	6. __________ bread	10. __________ fruit
3. __________ yogurt	7. __________ apple	11. __________ cheese
4. __________ egg	8. __________ cup of coffee	12. __________ beef

6. *some* o *any*?

Llene los espacios con *some* o *any*.

1. Excuse me, do you have __________ French wine?
2. We have __________ Californian wine, but we don't have __________ French wine.
3. Do we have __________ eggs in the refrigerator?
4. I'm sorry, but there isn't __________ fruit.
5. I'd like __________ cheese and __________ French bread.
6. I want __________ apples, but I don't want __________ oranges.

Texto en contexto

7. La carta de Betty

Betty le escribe una carta a su madre y le cuenta sobre las discusiones que ha tenido con su esposo Phil. Formule preguntas con las palabras que se dan a continuación y contéstelas en forma corta.

Phil and I had an argument yesterday - about food. He eats and eats and eats! And he never does any exercise. He's really big - in fact, he's fat! He always eats eggs and sausages and toast for breakfast, and he usually has a hamburger or a pizza for lunch. I buy yogurt and fruit and milk for him - then I open the refrigerator, and there's beer, and more hamburgers, and more pizza! He likes tennis, and swimming, and football - but only on the television. And he's fifty next year! What do I do?

1. yesterday/who/an/had/argument?

----

2. Phil/exercise/any/does/do?

----

3. he/a lot/breakfast/eat/for/does?

----

4. pizza/hamburgers/buys/and/who?

----

5. often/tennis/he/does/play?

----

6. fifty/is/he/when?

¡A escribir!

8. El desayuno y el almuerzo

Construya oraciones sobre lo que Bob, Jane, Phil y Betty toman para el desayuno y el almuerzo generalmente.

	Breakfast	**Lunch**
Bob	egg, toast, coffee or tea	soup or omelet
Jane	orange juice, yogurt, toast	sandwich
Phil	eggs,ham, toast, coffee or tea	hamburger or pizza
Betty	toast, tea	apple, cheese

Ejemplo: Bob usually has an egg, some toast, and some coffee or tea for breakfast. He usually has some soup or an omelet for lunch.

1. Jane ---------------------------------------
2. Phil ---------------------------------------
3. Betty ---------------------------------------

UNIDAD 11: Can you speak French?

En la unidad 11 hablaremos sobre lo que se puede o no se puede hacer y sobre diferentes profesiones. También aparecen ejercicios para pedir y dar explicaciones sobre algo, utilizando *why?* y *because.*

Juegos de palabras

1. Verbos

Relacione cada verbo con la frase apropiada.

1. drive	( )	a. a bicycle
2. speak	( )	b. an omelet
3. use	( )	c. a song
4. play	( )	d. a bus
5. make	( )	e. the guitar
6. ride	( )	f. a letter
7. sing	( )	g. French and German
8. type	( )	h. a word processor

De persona a persona

2. Sí, yo puedo

Jane quiere irse de Los Angeles por un tiempo, así que hoy ha ido a buscar trabajo a una compañía de turismo. Llene los espacios en blanco con un verbo apropiado de los que aparecen en el cuadro.

start
teach
use
speak (x2)
love
drive (x4)
type

Jane I can _________ , and I can _________ a word processor.

Mrs. Thomas That's not important. We have lots of secretaries. Can you _________ any foreign languages?

Jane Yes, I can _________ Spanish, and a little French and German.

Mrs. Thomas Good. Can you write them too?

Jane Yes, I can.

Mrs. Thomas And can you _________ ? Can you _________ a bus?

Jane A bus! No, I can't. I can _________ a car, but I can't _________ a bus.

Mrs. Thomas Don't worry - we can _________ you. Do you like hot weather?

Jane Yes. I was born in Ecuador - I _________ hot weather!

Mrs. Thomas Very good, very good. Would you like a job?

Jane As a secretary?

Mrs. Thomas No, as a tour guide. Would you like a job as a tour guide to Ecuador?
Jane Yes, I'd love it!
Mrs. Thomas Good. And one more question - can you __________ tomorrow?

Palabras mágicas

3. Trabajos

Formule preguntas con las palabras del cuadro, de tal modo que concuerden con las respuestas de la derecha.

cook type paint drive speak French play the piano sing

1. Can you play the piano? — Yes, in fact I'm a pianist.
2. ______________________ — Yes, in fact I'm an artist.
3. ______________________ — Yes, in fact I'm a French teacher.
4. ______________________ — Yes, in fact I'm a secretary.
5. ______________________ — Yes, in fact I'm a chef.
6. ______________________ — Yes, in fact I'm a bus driver.
7. ______________________ — Yes, in fact I'm an opera singer.

4. Profesiones u oficios

¿Cuántos profesiones u oficios puede Ud. encontrar?

L	S	M	D	O	R	P	C	E	E	D
O	A	E	E	S	L	O	H	P	N	O
F	C	P	N	U	R	S	E	A	G	C
F	T	I	T	V	E	T	F	I	I	T
P	O	L	I	C	E	M	A	N	N	O
E	R	O	S	O	W	A	I	T	E	R
L	I	T	T	P	O	N	B	E	E	E
L	R	E	P	O	R	T	E	R	R	S

El idioma en la mira

5. Preguntas con *Wh-*

Ejemplo: What can Jane play? ______ Who can play the guitar?
Jane can play the *guitar*. *Jane* can play the guitar.

1. ______
You can see the doctor *on Tuesday*.

2. ______
I can see *Bob* from the window.

3. ______
You can buy some vegetables *at the supermarket*.

4. ______
You can cook *omelets* for lunch.

5. ______
Betty and Phil can come to the party.

6. ______
Betty can sing *opera*.

6. Oraciones con *because*

Complete estas oraciones con *because* y una de las frases abajo.

1. I'm sorry, I can't play tennis tomorrow because I'm busy
2. I can't buy a new car because ______
3. Bob couldn't come to the party because ______
4. She didn't go swimming because ______
5. I couldn't make an omelet because ______
6. I can't go camping because ______
7. Jane couldn't eat her lunch because ______
8. He didn't go to the library because ______

a. He wasn't well.
b. I don't have a tent.
c. She wasn't hungry.
d. I don't have any money.
e. I'm busy.
f. It was closed.
g. I didn't have any eggs.
h. It was cold.

Texto en contexto

7. El mensaje de Jane

Lea el recado que le deja Jane a Bob y conteste las siguientes preguntas . Empiece cada una con *Because...*

> Sorry, but I can't meet you for lunch tomorrow - I've got a new job! In fact, I can't see you this week or next week at all - I'm really busy. I called you last night, but you weren't at home. Were you at the bar? Or with that foreign tourist? It's not important now. I don't really like Los Angeles any more - it's boring. Next week - Ecuador! I love Ecuador - it's fun, fun, fun. So goodbye Los Angeles, and goodbye Bob.
>
> Jane

1. Why can't she meet Bob for lunch tomorrow?

   ----

2. Why can't she see him next week?

   ----

3. Why didn't she tell him the news last night?

   ----

4. Why doesn't she like Los Angeles much any more?

   ----

5. Why does she like Ecuador? --

¡A escribir!

8. ¿Habla español?

	play tennis	speak Spanish	ski
Betty		yes - a little	not very well
Phil		yes - very well	
Andy	yes -very well	no	not at all
Linda	yes - a little		not at all

Ejemplo: Betty/ski Can Betty ski? No, she can't ski very well.

1. Phil/speak Spanish --
2. Andy/speak Spanish --
3. Betty/speak Spanish --
4. Andy and Linda/ski --
5. Andy/tennis --
6. Linda/speak Spanish --

UNIDAD 12: Review

En la Unidad 12 haremos una revisión del trabajo realizado desde la unidad 1 hasta la unidad 11.

1. Otra forma de decirlo

Enlace las oraciones que tienen significados semejantes.

1. I'm married.	( )	a. Are you hungry?
2. I'm a vegetarian.	( )	b. We went to a restaurant yesterday evening.
3. I live in Boston.	( )	c. Skiing is difficult.
4. Would you like something to eat?	( )	d. Did you speak to him yesterday evening?
5. Skiing isn't easy.	( )	e. They have a son and a daughter.
6. We all ate out last night.	( )	f. I'm not single.
7. They have two children.	( )	g. My address is 10 Broad Street, Boston.
8. Did you call him last night?	( )	h. I don't eat meat.

2. A, B O C?

Elija la respuesta correcta.

1. How do you do?
   a. I'm fine.
   b. How do you do?
   c. Thank you.

2. Would you like a drink?
   a. No, thank you.
   b. I'd like a drink, please.
   c. I like tea.

3. Are there any shops near your office?
   a. No, it isn't.
   b. Yes, there are.
   c. Yes, they're near.

4. Do you like your new boss?
   a. He likes me.
   b. I like it a lot.
   c. She's okay.

5. How much is that blue shirt?
   a. No, it's a green shirt.
   b. It's thirty dollars.
   c. There are three shirts.

6. Is the post office far from here?
   a. No, it's far.
   b. It's on the left.
   c. No, it's very near.

3. Los números

Escriba en el espacio en blanco la palabra correspondiente.

1. 1st ______
2. $4.50 ______
3. 16 ______
4. 60 ______
5. 10,500 ______
6. 3rd ______
7. 1984 ______
8. 75¢ ______

4. Los antónimos

Escriba al frente de cada palabra el antónimo correspondiente.

1. hot ______
2. always ______
3. bad ______
4. black ______
5. close ______
6. difficult ______
7. far ______
8. uncle ______
9. hello ______
10. single ______
11. men ______
12. summer ______

5. Preguntas

Haga preguntas que concuerden con estas respuestas.

1. ______
   They're 50¢ each.
2. ______
   I bought it yesterday.
3. ______
   It closes at 5:30.
4. ______
   Red.
5. ______
   She's 10.
6. ______
   Yes, I've got two sons and one daughter.

6. Tiempo pasado

Escriba al frente de cada verbo su tiempo pasado.

1. have ------------------------------
2. do ------------------------------
3. tell ------------------------------
4. speak ------------------------------
5. swim ------------------------------
6. come ------------------------------
7. go ------------------------------
8. meet ------------------------------
9. drink ------------------------------
10. drive ------------------------------

7. Formas negativas

Ponga estas frases en forma negativa.

Ejemplo: I wrote a letter to my mother. I didn't write a letter to my mother.

1. We went shopping yesterday. ------------------------------
2. The house has a big yard. ------------------------------
3. He really likes his new job. ------------------------------
4. I bought some fruit this morning. ------------------------------
5. He gets up at 7:00 every morning. ------------------------------
6. They went camping last year. ------------------------------

8. Oraciones en desorden

Ordene las palabras para formar oraciones.

1. size does what he ? shoes he take

----

2. is men's the the on floor second department

----

3. right our on house is second the

----

4. and family hotel a Betty in stayed her

----

5. cheese is refrigerator in there the any ?

----

6. tennis because can't I'm I play busy

----

9. Búsqueda de errores

Cada oración tiene un error. Identifíquelo y escriba la oración correctamente.

Ejemplo: I went ~~their~~ last week. I went there last week.

1. The library is close on Sunday. ____________________
2. He doesn't have some children. ____________________
3. I usually have a soup for lunch. ____________________
4. We all went to San Diego in train. ____________________
5. My sister and me went camping in Canada. ____________________
6. Excuse me, do you got any orange juice? ____________________

10. Crucigrama

Utilice las pistas para llenar el crucigrama.

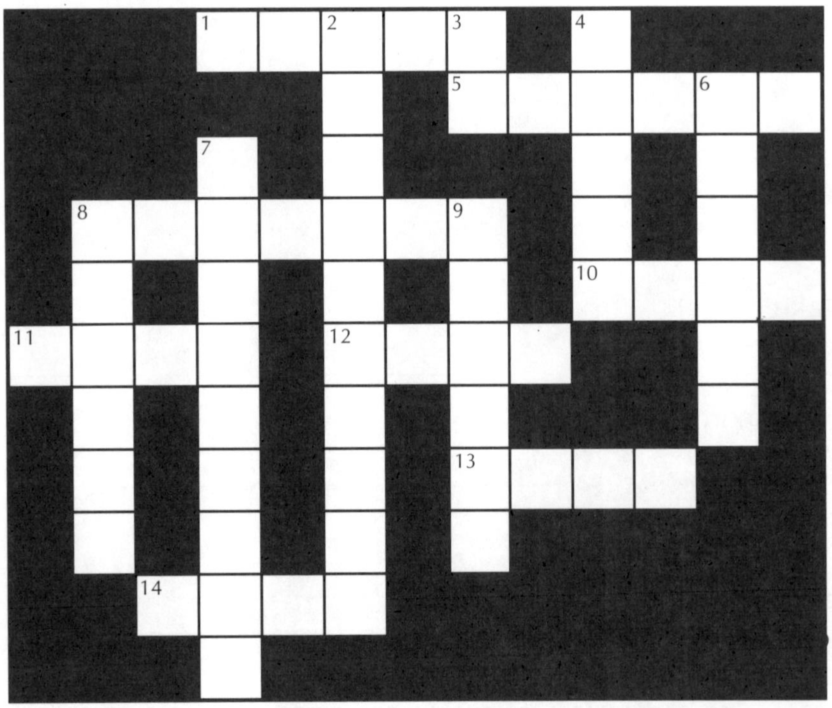

Across

1. How many days are there in a week?
5. A fruit, and a color
8. Saturday and Sunday
10. A street
11 Men wear these.
12. Your mother's sister
13. Make an omelet with these.
14. Small, green vegetables

Down:

2. Carrots and potatoes are these.
3. Opposite of yes.
4. You can drink this, or swim in it.
6. Is there a car in here?
7. Do you read this every day?
8. He works in a restaurant.
9. Evening meal.

UNIDAD 13: Who's who?

En la unidad 13 practicaremos la,manera de describir personas. También haremos algunos ejercicios de comparación.

Juegos de palabras

1. ¿Quién es quién?

Relacione las palabras con el dibujo correspondiente.

1. tall
2. fat
3. dark
4. fair
5. strong
6. old
7. happy
8. slim

De persona a persona

2. ¿Cómo es él?

Lea la conversación entre Betty y su esposo Phil. A continuación subraye *True* si la afirmación es verdadera y *False* si es falsa.

Phil	I saw that new reporter of yours in the bar last night. He was rather unhappy.
Betty	Really? Who's that?
Phil	I don't know his name. I saw him at your office party last week.
Betty	What does he look like?
Phil	Tall and slim. He has long, dark hair. He's about 30.
Betty	That's Bob Kushner. He has a big nose, but he's handsome. Is that him?
Phil	Yes, that's him. He wasn't very happy last night. And he drank a lot too.

Betty That's because his girlfriend has a new job - she went to Ecuador yesterday, as a tour guide.

Phil That attractive young woman? With the short hair? She always wears big earrings?

Betty Yes, that's right. Why? Do you know her?

1. Bob was at the bar last night. *True/False*
2. Phil was at the office party last night. *True/False*
3. Bob has dark hair. *True/False*
4. Bob is fat. *True/False*
5. Bob drank a lot last night, because he was very happy. *True/False*
6. Bob's girlfriend likes big earrings. *True/False*

P Palabras mágicas

3. Los opuestos

¿Cuál es el opuesto de las siguientes palabras?

1. sad	----------------------------	5. fair	----------------------------
2. young	----------------------------	6. tall	----------------------------
3. cheap	----------------------------	7. big	----------------------------
4. long	----------------------------	8. heavy	----------------------------

4. Partes del cuerpo

Escriba en cada espacio la parte del cuerpo señalada.

El idioma en la mira

5. Comparativos y superlativos

Complete el cuadro con el comparativo y el superlativo correspondientes.

Adjetivo	Comparativo	Superlativo
1. short		
2. old		
3. good		
4. long		
5. happy		
6. attractive		
7. heavy		
8. big		
9. easy		
10. slim		

6. ¡A ordenar palabras!

Ponga las palabras en el orden correcto para formar oraciones o preguntas.

1. Mount Everest/world/mountain/the/the/is/in/highest

   ----

2. Betty/sister/beautiful/more/is/her/than

   ----

3. longer/Bob/he/hair/than/has/

   ----

4. world/longest/the/the/in/what/is/river

   ----

5. is/family/his/tallest/Andy/the/in

   ----

6. car/more/mine/expensive/was/your/than

Texto en contexto

7. Una cita a ciegas

Joe, el amigo de Bob, le organiza una cita a ciegas con otra amiga, Jenny. A continuación se encuentra el mensaje que Bob le esribe a Jenny para confirmar donde y cuando se van a encontrar. Complete los espacios con una de las palabras del cuadro de la izquierda.

eyes
don't have
the same
long
wear
more
taller

Hi – Can we meet on Friday? How about The Bell, at 7:30? I'm ________ weight and height as Joe – but I'm ________ handsome! I'm also ________ than him. I have ________, black hair, and brown ________. I always ________ jeans and a black leather jacket. Sorry I ________ a photograph!

See you on Friday.

Bob Kushner

¡A escribir!

8. Conteste las preguntas

Conteste las siguientes preguntas con oraciones completas siguiendo el ejemplo.

Ejemplo: Who is the lightest?
Sue is the lightest.

	Enrique	Ray	Sue
Age	27	34	31
Height	6ft	5ft 10in	5ft 5in
Weight	145lbs	156lbs	110lbs
Hair	dark	dark	fair

1. Who is the heaviest? ________________
2. Who is the oldest? ________________
3. Who is the youngest? ________________
4. Who is the tallest? ________________
5. Who is younger than Sue? ________________
6. Who is shorter than Enrique? ________________
7. Who has darker hair than Sue? ________________

UNIDAD 14: Having a great time!

En esta unidad podremos hablar de lo que esta sucediendo en el momento. Describiremos el tiempo y hablaremos de sus consecuencias, utilizando *so*.

Juegos de palabras

1. ¿Qué tiempo hace?

Enlace las oraciones utilizando la partícula *so*.

1. It's snowing today	so... ( )	a. we can't ride our bicycles.
2. It's raining today	so... ( )	b. we can't see anything.
3. The sun is shining today	so... ( )	c. I'm wearing my hat and gloves.
4. It's foggy today	so... ( )	d. the children are all swimming in the sea.
5. It's windy today	so... ( )	e. I'm sitting in the yard.
6. It's very hot today	so... ( )	f. I'm carrying an umbrella.

De persona a persona

2. Viejos amigos

De visita en Ecuador, Jane llama a sus viejos amigos, Pete y Carmen. Complete los espacios en blanco en el diálogo con las palabras del cuadro.

visiting
working (x2)
cooking
cleaning
calling
washing
doing (x2)
living (x2)

Jane Hello, Pete? This is Jane, Jane Harris.

Pete Jane! How are you?!

Jane I'm fine. And you?

Pete Great. But where are you now? What are you _________ ? Are you _________ from the States? Or are you here in Quito?

Jane I'm in Quito.

Pete On vacation?

Jane No, I have a new job as a travel guide.

Pete You're _________ as a travel guide in Quito! Great. Are you _________ in Quito too?

Jane No, I'm not __________ in Quito I'm just __________ Ecuador for ten days with a tour. How about you? What are you __________ ?

Pete At the moment? Right now I'm __________ clothes and __________ the house.

Jane Where's Carmen?

Pete Carmen's __________ at the office today. Hey, are you free tonight? Would you like some dinner?

Jane At your house? Who's __________ it?

Pete I am.

Jane Okay, I'd love dinner! What time?

Palabras mágicas

3. Sobra una

Encierre en un círculo la palabra que no pertenece al grupo.

1. snow hot fog rain wind
2. working skiing swimming hiking skating
3. always usually sometimes often now
4. today this morning now week this evening
5. umbrella gloves hat scarf socks
6. newspaper book brochure magazine word processor

4. Encuentre el país

¿Adónde quiere ir Betty de vacaciones este año? Complete los espacios con la forma correcta del verbo.

1. Bob is ____ in a small apartment in Los Angeles.
2. Jane is ____ a postcard to her parents.
3. It's hot today, so we're ____ lots of water.
4. Steve is ____ as a waiter.
5. The children are all ____ in the sea.
6. Betty is just ____ her teeth.
7. Who is ____ that song?
8. Phil is ____ in a chair by the pool.
9. They're ____ by train and bus.

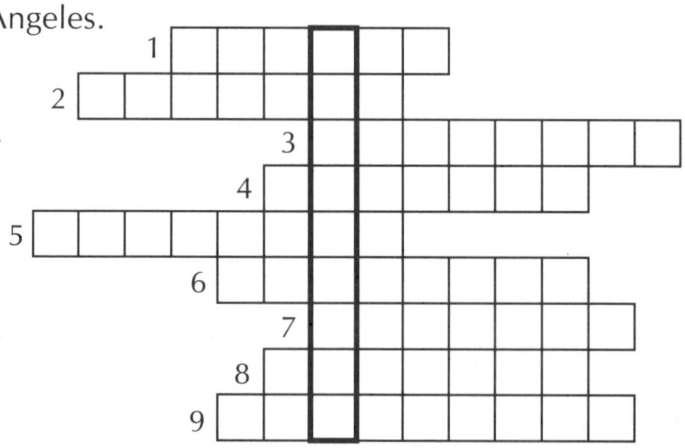

El idioma en la mira

5. ¿El presente simple o el presente continuo (*-ing*)?

Llene los espacios utilizando el verbo entre paréntesis en presente simple o en presente continuo.

1. (take) I usually ________ a shower in the mornings, but this morning ________ a bath.
2. (wear) She usually ________ a dress or a suit to the office, but today ________ jeans.
3. (drive) Phil usually ________ the family car on vacation, but today Betty ________ it.
4. (travel) We usually ________ by train, but this summer ________ by bus.
5. (cook) Carmen usually ________ dinner on the weekend, but today Pete ________ it.
6. (go) The children usually ________ swimming on Saturday mornings, but this morning ________ skating.

6. *So* o *because*?

Escriba de nuevo estas oraciones uniéndolas con *so* o *because* según corresponda.

Ejemplo: It was Betty's birthday. We all went out to a restaurant.

It was Betty's birthday, so we all went out to a restaurant.

1. We're camping. We don't really like staying in hotels.

   ____

2. Today is my birthday. I'm having a party.

   ____

3. I'm staying at home today. It's raining.

   ____

4. I couldn't go on vacation last year. I didn't have any money.

   ____

5. The children are all sleeping. It's very quiet.

   ____

6. I love skiing. I always go to Canada or Chile for my vacation.

   ____

Texto en contexto

7. La tarjeta postal de Jane

Esta es una postal que Jane escribió a sus padres. Construya preguntas que concuerden con estas respuestas.

Ejemplo: Where is she sitting? By the pool.

1. ________________ A cold beer.
2. ________________ Thirty-five.
3. ________________ Yesterday.
4. ________________ Three.
5. ________________ No, he isn't.

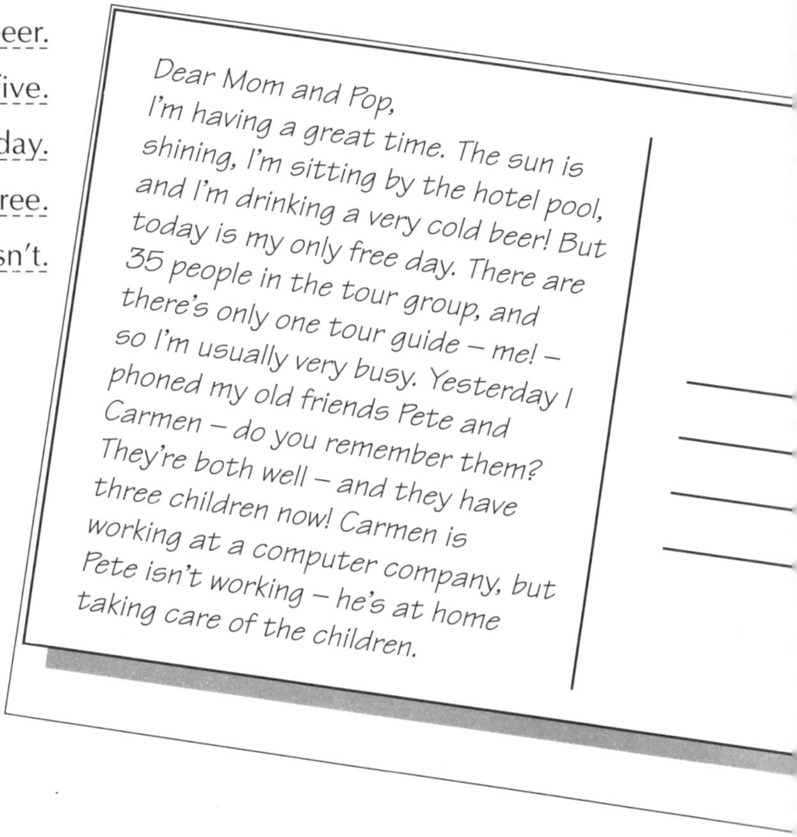
Dear Mom and Pop,
I'm having a great time. The sun is shining, I'm sitting by the hotel pool, and I'm drinking a very cold beer! But today is my only free day. There are 35 people in the tour group, and there's only one tour guide – me! – so I'm usually very busy. Yesterday I phoned my old friends Pete and Carmen – do you remember them? They're both well – and they have three children now! Carmen is working at a computer company, but Pete isn't working – he's at home taking care of the children.

¡A escribir!

8. *He is, he isn't*

Construya oraciones utilizando las palabras clave siguiendo el ejemplo.

Ejemplo: Pablo and Linda aren't playing tennis, they're playing golf.

Pablo & Linda	play	~~tennis~~	golf
1. Betty	wear	~~suit~~	dress
2. Jane	write	~~postcard~~	letter
3. Bob & his friend	drink	~~wine~~	juice
4. Andy	work	~~as a waiter~~	as a mailman
5. Linda	–	~~ski~~	skate
6. Pop	read	~~magazine~~	newspaper

UNIDAD 15: We'd love to!

En la unidad 15 practicaremos cómo hablar sobre el futuro. También haremos planes y daremos sugerencias.

Juegos de palabras

1. Las invitaciones

Relacione las invitaciones o comentarios de la izquierda con las respuestas de la derecha.

1. Would you like to go to the theater on Saturday evening?	( )	a. Yes, I'm playing tennis.
2. Are you free this evening?	( )	b. Great! What day is it?
3. How about watching that movie on TV tonight?	( )	c. Never mind.
4. How about 7:30 in front of the station?	( )	d. I'd love to! What's on?
5. Are you doing anything on Sunday?	( )	e. Good idea.
6. I'd like to invite you to my birthday party.	( )	f. Fine. See you there.
7. Sorry, but I'm teaching all day on Tuesday.	( )	g. Why? What's happening?

De persona a persona

2. Una invitación de cumpleaños

Complete los espacios en blanco escogiendo la frase más apropiada del cuadro de la derecha.

Kate Hello, Phil? This is Kate. Can I speak to Betty, please? Is she there?

Phil Hi, Kate. Yes, she is. (1) __________ – she's out in the yard. (shouting) BETTY! KATE IS ON THE PHONE FOR YOU! She's just coming, Kate.

Kate Thanks. .....Betty, hi! (2) __________ . Are you busy?

Betty No, it's okay. I'm just doing some work in the yard. What is it?

Kate Well, are you free next Tuesday evening?

Betty (3) __________ .What's the date?

Is that okay?
We'd love to.
By the way,
I don't know.
I think so.
Never mind.
Hold on a minute,
Sorry to bother you.

Kate	The 2nd – June 2nd. It's John's birthday and some friends are going out to dinner at that new Japanese restaurant. Would you and Phil like to come?
Betty	(4) __________ . Hold on a minute – I'm just checking my agenda. Yes, I'm free. Oh, Phil is going to a meeting in San Diego that day. (5) __________ I can come!
Kate	Good.
Betty	Where and when are we meeting?
Kate	At our house, about 6:30. (6) __________ .
Betty	Yes, fine. I'm looking forward to it. (7) __________ , what are you giving him for his birthday?
Kate	(8) __________ I'm thinking about a small camera, or maybe a watch.

Palabras mágicas

3. Los meses

Partiendo de estas abreviaturas escriba los meses del año y añada los que faltan. Escriba en el espacio el número de orden de cada mes.

1.	____	Mar.	______________________	7.	____	Feb.	______________________
2.	____	Nov.	______________________	8.	____	Oct.	______________________
3.	____	Apr.	______________________	9.	____	Sept.	______________________
4.	____	Jan.	______________________	10.	____		______________________
5.	____	Dec.	______________________	11.	____		______________________
6.	____	Aug.	______________________	12.	____		______________________

4. ¿Qué tal si vamos a...?

A continuación aparecen algunos lugares o eventos a los que Ud. podría ser invitado. Ordene las letras y descubra que lugares son.

1. oivem ______________________
2. heatter ______________________
3. unseattarr ______________________
4. talebl ______________________
5. tryap ______________________
6. docis ______________________
7. roccent ______________________
8. esummu ______________________

El idioma en la mira

5. *How about....?*

Transforme estas invitaciones en sugerencias siguiendo el ejemplo.

Ejemplo: Would you like to play tennis on Tuesday?

How about playing tennis on Tuesday?

1. Would you like to see a movie on Wednesday?

----

2. Would you like to go for a walk this afternoon?

----

3. Would you like to play golf this Sunday?

----

4. Would you like to go camping in August?

----

5. Would you like to stay at home this evening?

----

6. Would you like to have a party on your birthday?

----

6. *Is/are* o *do/does?*

Haga preguntas y forme oraciones utilizando *is/are* o *do/does.*

Ejemplo: What/you/usually/watch/TV? What do you usually watch on TV?

What/watch/TV/this evening? What are you watching on TV this evening?

1. When/Bob and Jenny/go/the movies? ----------
2. How long/Jane/stay/Ecuador? ----------
3. What/you/usually/do/weekends? ----------
4. Phil/always/clean/car/Sundays? ----------
5. What/they/see/theater/tonight? ----------
6. Betty and Phil/speak/French? ----------
7. Bob/go/Spain/June? ----------
8. Phil/come/ballet/Tuesday? ----------

Texto en contexto

7. La parrillada

Los amigos de Jane, Pete y Carmen le han organizado una parrillada; a continuación verá Ud. una invitación para otros amigos suyos. Escriba de nuevo la tarjeta poniendo las lineas en órden.

Dear Miguel,

1. coming, and Julie and Ian are coming too – with their
2. afternoon? An old friend is visiting from
3. her. We've got lots of food and beer, so you just
4. seeing you here – from about 2:00.
5. bring the family, and your swimming things. The Thompsons are
6. Hi, how are you? Here's an invitation – would you
7. Los Angeles, and we're having a barbecue for
8. like to come around to our house on Sunday
9. three dogs! We're looking forward to

Pete and Carmen

¡A escribir!

8. Un partido de tenis

Dos amigos tratan de organizar un partido de tenis. Conteste las siguientes preguntas con base en el calendario, siguiendo el ejemplo.

Ejemplo: How about Monday evening? I'm sorry, but I'm going to see a movie with my family on Monday evening.

MAY

Mon	Tue	Wed	Thur	Fri	Sat	Sun
3 6:30 to movie with family	4 10:00- doctor 6:00 visit Mom	5 2:00: golf with Tom party at Betty's	6 Take care of children	7 paint the bathroom	8 9:30 take children to children's theater	9 church tea at Mom's

1. How about Tuesday evening? ______________________
2. How about the afternoon of the fifth? ______________________
3. How about Thursday morning or afternoon? ______________________
4. How about May 7th? ______________________
5. How about Saturday morning? ______________________
6. How about Sunday morning? ______________________

UNIDAD 16: Do you come here often?

En esta unidad encontraremos ejemplos de conversaciones, y ejercicios pidiendo y dando permiso para hacer algo. También hablaremos sobre la frecuencia con que realizamos ciertas actividades.

Juegos de palabras

1. Yo también

Enlace cada enunciado de la izquierda con una de las expresiones de la derecha.

1. I really like ballet.
2. I'm learning the guitar.
3. I don't enjoy sports.
4. I was busy yesterday.
5. I'm not doing anything this weekend.
6. I went to the theater last night.
7. I didn't give Jim a birthday present.
8. My parents live in Bogotá.
9. My apartment is really expensive.

( ) a. I was, too.
( ) b. I'm not, either.
( ) c. Mine do, too.
( ) d. I did.
( ) e. I did, too.
( ) f. I don't.
( ) g. Mine is, too.
( ) h. I am, too.
( ) i. I don't, either.

De persona a persona

2. Una conversación agradable

Rellene los espacios con *a, the* o con una X si ninguno de aquellos es necesario.

Jenny This is _________ nice place, isn't it?. Do you come here often?

Bob Yes – two or three times _________ week. How about you? What do you like doing in your free time?

Jenny Let's see. I like _________ singing, and I'm learning _________ guitar. I have _________ lessons every Tuesday and Saturday. And I like _________ painting. And I go to _________ movies a lot, too.

Bob Hey, you're busy, aren't you! Do you ever go to _________ theater?

Jenny Yes, I love _________ theater.

Bob I do, too. In fact, I've two tickets for _________ Arts Theater for _________ Friday evening – would you like to go?

Jenny Yes, thank you, I'd like that.

Bob Good. Let's have another drink. Oh, just _________ minute. Uh – do you mind if we go to _________ different bar?

Jenny No, I don't mind. But why? And who's that strange woman over there? What's she doing? Why is she looking at you?

Bob It's nothing. I don't know her. Come on. Let's go.

Palabras mágicas

3. Categorías

Agrupe estas palabras por categorías.

a telephone, a soccer game, Spanish, a calendar, a camera, TV, movies, cooking, a computer, painting, plays, the guitar, a video, a clock, money, photography, typing

1. Things to learn ______________________

2. Things to watch ______________________

3. Things to see ______________________

4. ¿Qué es?

Escoja una de las palabras mencionadas en las categorías anteriores para completar las oraciones.

1. __________ is a sport.
2. A __________ is a musical instrument.
3. __________ is a language.
4. A __________ takes photographs.
5. A __________ shows the date.
6. A __________ shows the time.

El idioma en la mira

5. Preguntas con 'talon'

Complete estas oraciones añadiendo una cláusula 'talon', siguiendo el ejemplo.

Ejemplo: They're going out tonight, aren't they?

1. You're Japanese, ____________
2. You come here every week, ____________
3. It's windy today, ____________
4. They went to Chile last year, ____________
5. You can play the guitar, ____________
6. He comes to this club often, ____________
7. You don't like Bob, ____________
8. That was a good party, ____________

6. Pidamos permiso

Pida permiso a alguien para hacer algo. Empiece con *Do you mind if...?* como en el ejemplo.

Ejemplo: You want to use somebody's telephone. Do you mind if I use your telephone?

1. You want to listen to the radio. ______________________
2. You want to call somebody at the office. ______________________
3. You want to read somebody's newspaper. ______________________
4. You want to borrow somebody's camera. ______________________
5. You want to sit next to somebody. ______________________
6. You're cold. The window is open. ______________________
7. It's hot. The door is closed. ______________________

7. Dando permiso

Relacione estas respuestas con las preguntas del ejercicio 6.

Ejemplo: Do you mind if I use your telephone?

Of course not, go ahead. Who are you calling?

Give permission	Refuse permission
Of course not, go ahead. Who are you calling?	
a. No, of course not. It's cold, isn't it?	e. Yes, I do. Please only call me at home.
b. Not at all. Please sit down.	f. Well, there's no film in it.
c. No, of course I don't mind. What's on?	g. I'm sorry – I'm reading it myself.
d. No, please go ahead.	

Texto en contexto

8.¿Con qué frecuencia...?

Después de leer esta descripción apunte en el diario las actividades que esta persona realiza con regularidad.

I'm very busy, really. I have a part-time job as an English teacher, and I teach on Monday, Tuesday and Friday mornings. I go swimming every Tuesday and Friday evening, but I have a dancing class on the first Friday of every month, so I can't swim then. I go camping every year with some friends, and this year we're going to Peru, so we're taking Spanish classes at the moment – we only study once a week, on Wednesday mornings, so we don't learn much. And I can't go next week because I'm going to the dentist (I see him once every six months). My mother comes to stay with me once a month, usually the first weekend, but this month I changed it to the second weekend, because I'm going to a party on Saturday evening.

	JUNE
M 1	
T 2	
W 3	
T 4	
F 5	
S 6	
S 7	

	JUNE
M 8	
T 9	
W 10	
T 11	
F 12	
S 13	
S 14	

¡A escribir!

9. ¿Alguna vez...?

Conteste estas preguntas acerca de Ud. mismo.

Ejemplo: Do you ever go camping? Yes, I go camping about twice a year.

or No, I never go camping.

1. Do you ever go skiing? ______
2. Do you ever listen to opera? ______
3. Do you ever speak Portuguese? ______
4. Do you ever drink whiskey? ______
5. Do you ever ride a bicycle? ______
6. Do you ever wear jeans? ______
7. Do you ever travel overseas? ______
8. Do you ever stay in a hotel? ______

UNIDAD 17: I'm going to be busy!

En la unidad 17 practicaremos el tiempo futuro, haremos predicciones y pediremos más información.

Juegos de palabras

1. Construcción de oracion

Construya oraciones utilizando elementos de las tres columnas.

1. I'm going to listen	about	go to a movie.
2. They're going to get	to	me?
3. Why is he looking	to	Bob, please?
4. We're going to go	up	in that letter?
5. I'd love	about	tonight.
6. Can I speak.	at	the radio.
7. What are you going to write	to	at 7:30.

De persona a persona

2. Una riña

Betty habla con su hijo Andy. Escriba las frases en el orden correcto para descubrir el motivo de la riña.

1. **Andy** No, I'm not going to pass, but it doesn't matter.
2. **Andy** I'm not going to get a job.
3. **Andy** No, not yet.
4. **Andy** I'm not going to college. I'm going to travel to Europe and then Canada.
5. **Andy** I'm not doing anything. Why?
6. **Betty** Not get a job? Well, what are you going to study at college?
7. **Betty** Why aren't you studying? Your exams are next month! What about your future!? Are you going to pass your exams?
8. **Betty** Andy, what are you doing in your room?
9. **Betty** Why doesn't it matter? What's going to happen after your exams? What job are you going to do?
10. **Betty** What?! And where are you going to get the money from? What are you going to do there? Why didn't you tell me? Did you tell your father?

Palabras mágicas

3. ¿Cuál es el verbo más apropiado?

Escoja el verbo más apropiado para cada oración.

1. Be quiet – I'm *listening to/hearing* the news on the radio.
2. Are Betty and Phil going to *come/go* to our party?
3. When are you going to *speak/tell* your husband about this?
4. Did you *see/look* at that movie on television last night? It was really good.
5. Do you mind if I *carry/bring* a friend to the concert?
6. I'm sorry, but I don't *understand/know* the question.

El idioma en la mira

4. Formulación de preguntas

Conteste a estos comentarios utilizando *going to*, de acuerdo con el ejemplo.

Ejemplo: We're going overseas this year.
(where/go) Really? Where are you going to go?

1. Bob is buying a new car this month.
(what kind) ____________________

2. We're painting the bathroom next week.
(what color) ____________________

3. I'm taking Jenny to the theater on Saturday night.
(what/see) ____________________

4. Pete and Carmen are moving house next month.
(where) ____________________

5. Betty is having a small dinner party on Friday.
(who/invite) ____________________

6. Hey, I've got a new job!
(when/start) ____________________

5. *Somebody* o *anybody*?

Complete las oraciones utilizando *somebody, something, somewhere, anything, anybody, anywhere.*

1. I'm not going to the party – there isn't going to be __________ interesting there.
2. Hush – I'm watching __________ interesting on the TV.
3. We don't have much money, so we're not going to go __________ this year.
4. Is __________ coming for a drink?
5. Betty's office is __________ in Greenwood.
6. Bob is going to give me __________ really expensive for my birthday.
7. Betty? Are you there? __________ is on the phone for you.
8. I'm so hungry – is there __________ in the refrigerator?

Texto en contexto

6. Predicción del futuro

Lea el horóscopo y corrija las siguientes oraciones acerca del mismo.

Your horoscope for this month.

Work:
This is not going to be a good month for you, so be careful! You're going to have some problems with colleagues at the beginning of the month, and money problems at the end of the month.

Love:
You're going to hear from an old friend – maybe a letter, maybe a telephone call, and this is going to cause problems with your partner – he's going to be jealous. There are going to be some arguments.

Health:
It's going to be a busy month socially – lots of parties and invitations, so take care of your health! You're going to need lots of exercise, sleep and a healthy diet.

Ejemplo: You're going to have a good month for work.

No, I'm not. I'm going to have a bad month for work.

1. There are going to be problems with money at the beginning of the month.

2. There's going to be news from the family.

3. Your partner is going to be happy.

4. There are going to be arguments with your boss.

5. It's going to be a quiet month socially.

6. You're not going to need much exercise.

¡A escribir!

7. Los propósitos de Linda

El año pasado Linda, la hija de Betty, escribió una lista de sus ambiciones en su diario secreto, pero ahora ha cambiado de opinión sobre la mayoría de ellas. Utilizando las siguientes anotaciones escriba su nueva lista de propósitos.

Ejemplo: marry – Mario (Steve)

I'm not going to marry Mario, I'm going to marry Steve.

1. learn - ~~guitar~~ piano
2. become - ~~teacher~~ engineer
3. live - ~~Canada~~ Brazil
4. drive - ~~Mercedes~~ Porsche
5. be - ~~beautiful~~ rich
6. have - ~~dogs~~ horses

UNIDAD 18: Round trip, please.

En esta unidad practicaremos comprando boletos, obteniendo información sobre los horarios de trenes, pidiendo que información importante sea repetida y solicitando información de manera cortés.

Juegos de palabras

1. Motivos

Relacione las preguntas con las respuestas apropiadas.

1. Why are you going to San Francisco?	( )	a. To reserve a room for a friend.
2. Why are you going to the sports center?	( )	b. To change some money.
3. Why are you going to the bus station?	( )	c. To see my parents.
4. Why are you going to the Station Hotel?	( )	d. To play tennis.
5. Why are you going to the airport?	( )	e. To get two tickets to Peoria.
6. Why are you going to the bank?	( )	f. To meet a friend from Miami.

De persona a persona

2. Comprando boletos de tren

Jenny va con Bob a San Francisco para visitar a sus padres. Ahora se encuentran en la estación de trenes comprando los boletos. Complete su conversación llenando los espacios con palabras o frases del cuadro de la derecha.

includes
returning
owe
platform
how much
time
round-trips
stay

Clerk Can I help you?

Jenny Yes, could I have two __________ to San Francisco, please?

Clerk Do you want round-trip tickets? Are you __________ from San Francisco today?

Jenny Yes, we are – two round-trip tickets, please.

Clerk There you are. That's $168.80, please.

Jenny Sorry, __________ ?

Clerk $168.80. That __________ the seat reservation.

Jenny Thanks. Could you tell me the __________ of the next train, please?

Clerk Let me see – the next San Francisco train is at 9:27, from ___________ 3.

Jenny Thank you. Come on, Bob.

Bob But I want to _________ in Los Angeles today, and rest a little, and meet my friends, and go to the beach. Why are we going to San Francisco today?

Jenny You know why – to meet my parents. Come on. And you __________ me $84.40.

Palabras mágicas

3 *Want* o *want to?*

Tache la palabra TO cuando ésta no sea necesaria.

1. Bob WANTS TO stay in Los Angeles today.
2. I'm going to the bank because I WANT TO exchange some traveler's checks.
3. Do you WANT TO a one-way or a round-trip?
4. I don't like buses - I WANT TO go by train.
5. Andy WANTS TO a car for his eighteenth birthday.
6. You owe me $20, and I WANT TO it now, please!
7. Where do you WANT TO go tonight?
8. I don't WANT TO any more coffee, thank you.

El idioma en la mira

4. Obteniendo información

Imagine que no entiende Ud. o que no puede oír lo que alguien dice. Pida que le repitan la información necesaria.

Ejemplo: The next flight to Tokyo is on *Wednesday*. I'm sorry - when?

1. The next bus to San Diego is *that blue one* over there. ______________
2. Could I have two one-way tickets *to Birmingham*, please? ______________
3. Mr. Jones? You had a telephone call *from Mr. Thomas*. ______________
4. A single room is *$32.00* a night. ______________
5. The next train to Vancouver is from *platform 2*. ______________

6. I'd like *three* round-trip tickets to Boston, please. ________________

7. The train arrives in New York at *12:35*. ________________

8. The plane is going to be late, because of *fog in Chicago*. ________________

5. Preguntas cortesas – *Could I ...?*

Lea las situaciones siguientes y construya respuestas apropiadas empezando con *Could ...?*

Ejemplo: You want to know the time of the next bus to San Diego.

Could you tell me the time of the next bus to San Diego, please?

1. Somebody is speaking very quickly – you don't understand.

____

2. You want two round-trip tickets to Chicago.

____

3. You want to know the way to the station.

____

4. You are on a plane, and you want some water.

____

5. You want your taxi driver to stop just here.

____

6. You want to write something, but you don't have a pen – the person next to you has one.

Texto en contexto

6. El diario de Jane

Jane hace breves anotaciones en su diario, sobre cada lugar en donde se ha quedado el grupo. Estudie las siguientes anotaciones y escríbalas de nuevo en forma de oraciones completas.

Ejemplo: Stayed in terrible hotel last night.
We stayed in a terrible hotel last night.

Stayed in terrible hotel last night. (1) Everyone in tour group very angry. (2) No double or twin rooms, and no showers! (3) Rooms dirty, and food in restaurant not good. (4) Wanted to find different hotel but too late. (5) Had argument with hotel manager – not a very nice man. (6) But all back to the States tomorrow! (7) Flight arrives L.A. 2:30 afternoon.

¡A escribir!

7. ¿A qué hora?

Construya diálogos sobre el horario, como en el ejemplo.

	New York	Stanford CT	Providence RI	Boston
	05:04	06:19	07:30	08:50
(1)	06:57	08:12	09:23	10:45
	07:42	08:57	10:08	11:20
(2)	08:12	09:27	10:38	11:52
	10:12	11:27	12:38	14:00

Ejemplo:

Passenger: Could you tell me the time of the next train from Stanford to Boston, please?

Station clerk: Yes, it leaves at six nineteen.

Passenger: And how long does it take?

Station clerk: It takes two hours and thirty-one minutes.

1. **Passenger:**
Station clerk:
Passenger:
Station clerk:

2. **Passenger:**
Station clerk:
Passenger:
Station clerk:

UNIDAD 19: I feel terrible.

Esta unidad trata de la salud y el ejercicio físico. Podremos hablar sobre cómo nos sentimos, nombrar las partes del cuerpo y también dar consejos para mejorar la salud.

Juegos de palabras

1. ¿Qué hace Ud. cuando tiene frío?

Enlace las dos partes para formar oraciones completas.

1. When I feel cold,	( )	a. I go to bed early.
2. When I feel lonely,	( )	b. I go to the sports center.
3. When I feel tired,	( )	c. I always drink water or juice.
4. When I feel hungry,	( )	d. I put on an extra sweater.
5. When I feel overweight,	( )	e. I make a cheese sandwich.
6. When I feel thirsty,	( )	f. I call my best friend.

De persona a persona

2. Pareces cansado

Jane regresó ayer de su viaje a Ecuador y hoy, al ir de compras, se encuentra con Bob. Complete el diálogo, llenando los espacios con la forma apropiada del verbo. Utilice la forma afirmativa o negativa de acuerdo con los signos (+) (-).

Bob Jane! Welcome back! How (be+) __________ the trip? You (look+) __________ tired.

Jane Yes, I am. We (have+) __________ a wonderful time, but it's a long trip back from Ecuador. I'm a bit jet-lagged. By the way, you look terrible! What (happen+) __________ ?

Bob I feel terrible. I have a headache, my stomach (hurt+) __________ , and I (can-) __________ sleep last night.

Jane Is it a hangover? Or have you got flu? Why don't you go home and go to bed?

Bob I can't – I (meet+) __________ someone in the bar at 7:30.

Jane A woman?

Bob Yes. In fact, I think she's the problem. Yesterday she (take+) __________ me to San Francisco, and I met her parents. We (have+) __________ lunch there, but her mother is a terrible cook. The food was awful, and I (be+) __________ sick on the train back. It was a horrible day. I (want-) __________ to see her any more.

Palabras mágicas

3. Las partes del cuerpo

Ordene las letras para encontrar los nombres de las diferentes partes del cuerpo y señálelos en el dibujo.

1. mathocs ----------------
2. edah ----------------
3. swirt ----------------
4. gle ----------------
5. dnah ----------------
6. neke ----------------
7. klean ----------------
8. otof ----------------
9. below ----------------
10. dyob ----------------

4. *Look* o *look like*?

Tache la palabra *like* cuando ésta no sea necesaria.

1. Jane LOOKS LIKE her father, doesn't she?
2. Felipe is an accountant, but he doesn't LOOK LIKE one.
3. I LOOK LIKE so fat in this dress!
4. Betty LOOKED LIKE a bit sick yesterday – is she okay?
5. Is that your brother? You don't LOOK LIKE him at all.

El idioma en la mira

5. Consejos

Dé un consejo apropiado como respuesta a estos comentarios. Empiece con *Why don't you ...?*

Ejemplo: My eyes hurt. (wear your glasses) Why don't you wear your glasses?

1. I've got a headache. (take aspirin) --
2. I have a horrible toothache. (go dentist) --

3. I feel so cold. (put on sweater)
4. I feel terrible. (see doctor)
5. I feel so tired today. (go to bed early)
6. I've got a pain in my knee. (sit down)
7. I'm so overweight. (go on diet)
8. I'm so unfit. (get more exercise)

6. Oraciones en desorden

Ordene las palabras para construir oraciones.

1. bored/to/I/I/feel/the/go/when/club/
2. see/why/doctor/a/you/don't/?
3. like/Bob/brother/look/doesn't/his
4. club/going/new/I'm/sports/to/that/join/
5. look/you/today/well/don't/very
6. headache/and/hurt/I/my/have/feet/a

Texto en contexto

7. Problemas de peso

Lea esta carta enviada a una revista. Corrija la información que aparece a continuación.

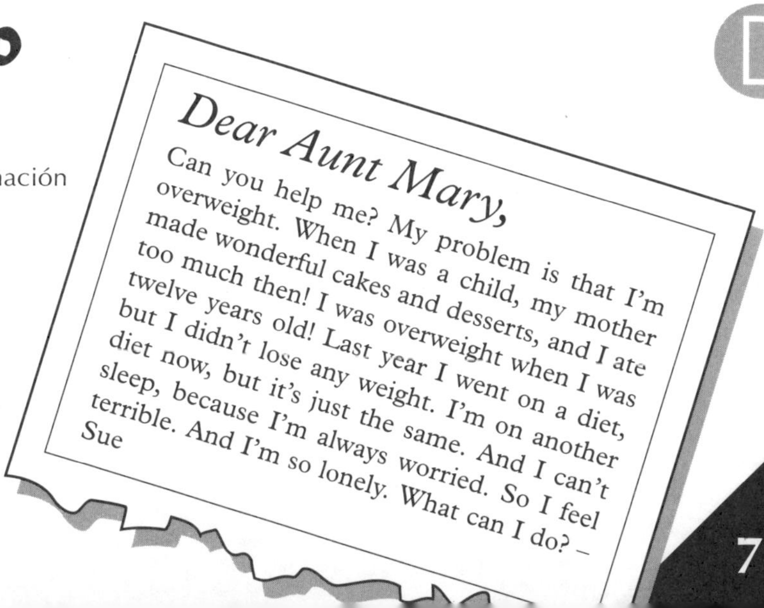

Dear Aunt Mary,

Can you help me? My problem is that I'm overweight. When I was a child, my mother made wonderful cakes and desserts, and I ate too much then! I was overweight when I was twelve years old! Last year I went on a diet, but I didn't lose any weight. I'm on another diet now, but it's just the same. And I can't sleep, because I'm always worried. So I feel terrible. And I'm so lonely. What can I do? – Sue

Dear Sue,

When you are overweight, diet is very important, but exercise is important too. Do you do any exercise? Why don't you join a sports club, or an exercise class? You can meet lots of interesting people when you do sports. When you do exercise, you feel better, and you look better. Good luck.

Aunt Mary

Ejemplo: Sue's mother was a bad cook.

No, she wasn't. She was a good cook.

1. Sue didn't eat much when she was a child.

____

2. She lost a lot of weight when she went on a diet.

____

3. She feels terrible, because she's always worried.

____

4. When you're overweight, diet and exercise aren't very important.

____

5. You meet lots of boring people when you do sports.

____

6. You look terrible when you do exercise.

____

¡A escribir!

8. *When I was 12,...*

Construya oraciones utilizando esta información acerca de la vida de alguien. Empiece con *When I ....*

Ejemplo: 12 years old, broke leg When I was 12 years old, I broke my leg.

1. camping in Canada, rained every day

____

2. at college, wore glasses

____

3. lived in San Diego, went jogging every day

____

4. worked as gardener, really fit!

____

5. worked as waiter, got really fat

____

UNIDAD 20: Have you ever ...?

En la unidad 20 hablaremos sobre nuestras experiencias y la duración de los eventos.

Juegos de palabras

1. *Hasn't/haven't*

Enlace las oraciones que tengan el mismo sentido.

1. It's still raining.	( )	a. We've drunk it.
2. We're still living in Los Angeles.	( )	b. I've forgotten it.
3. I'm still reading the newspaper.	( )	c. She hasn't gone home yet.
4. There isn't any more wine.	( )	d. It's gone.
5. Betty is still at the office.	( )	e. It hasn't stopped.
6. Andy is still in bed.	( )	f. We haven't moved.
7. I can't remember his name.	( )	g. I haven't finished it yet.
8. The train left five minutes ago.	( )	h. He hasn't gotten up yet.

De persona a persona

2. Todavía no se ha levantado

Es sábado por la mañana y Betty ha ido de compras. Al regresar a casa encuentra a su hija Linda tomando café. Lea la conversación y determina si las siguientes afirmaciones son verdaderas o falsas.

Betty Where's Andy?

Linda I don't know. I haven't seen him this morning.

Betty What? Hasn't he gotten up yet? It's nearly lunchtime!

Linda He went to the disco last night, didn't he? He's probably tired.

Betty I don't care. ANDY? ANDY! GET UP! IT'S LUNCHTIME! Linda, have you cleaned up your room?

Linda No, not yet. I'm going to do it this afternoon.

Betty But you're going to the jazz festival this afternoon.

Linda I know, I know.

Betty Have you taken the dog out for a walk? You haven't, have you!

Linda No, I haven't. Sorry, I forgot.

Betty You forgot? Linda, what has happened to you? You forget so many things now. Have there been any phone calls?

Linda Yes, there were three calls, but they were all for me.

1. Andy is still in bed. *True/False*
2. Linda saw Andy at a disco. *True/False*
3. Linda hasn't cleaned up her room. *True/False*
4. Linda hasn't taken the dog out. *True/False*
5. They have eaten lunch. *True/False*
6. There haven't been any phone calls for Betty this morning. *True/False*

P Palabras mágicas

3. *For* o *since?*

Llene los espacios con *for* o *since.*

1. We've lived in New York __________ 1982.
2. Betty has been on a diet __________ her birthday.
3. Betty and Phil have been married __________ twenty-six years.
4. Bob looks terrible – he's had a cold __________ last Tuesday.
5. I've only known Bob __________ a month.
6. Pat has worked overseas __________ eighteen months.
7. It's been raining __________ 8:00 this morning.
8. Linda has been in the bathroom __________ an hour!

4. ¿Alguna vez has ...?

Algunas palabras se han mezclado en estas frases. Escríbalas de nuevo correctamente.

1. Have you ever eaten your leg? ____
2. Have you ever been to a golf? ____
3. Have you ever ridden a department store? ____
4. Have you ever played Australian wine? ____

5. Have you ever lived in a horse? --

6. Have you ever drunk Japanese food? --

7. Have you ever broken your apartment? --

8. Have you ever worked in a pop festival? --

El idioma en la mira

5. Cuadro de palabras

¿Puede Ud. encontrar el participio de los verbos que aparecen en el cuadro de palabras? El primero ya ha sido resuelto.

take do receive move
hear stop forget meet
see sing read go leave
write eat complain drink

S	E	L	I	T	O	O	J	R	E	A	D
R	A	S	U	D	D	I	H	E	A	R	D
O	T	L	S	S	E	E	N	C	A	C	E
L	E	F	T	C	C	H	N	E	L	F	T
O	N	C	O	M	P	L	A	I	N	E	D
I	S	S	P	M	N	B	O	V	L	W	O
P	G	A	P	R	T	A	K	E	N	R	N
M	O	V	E	D	G	N	A	D	J	I	E
H	N	D	D	R	U	N	K	C	M	T	L
V	E	B	O	N	N	E	C	M	E	T	O
Y	E	K	F	O	R	G	O	T	T	E	N
E	D	I	F	T	H	A	R	S	U	N	G

6. Escoja el tiempo correcto

Escoja el tiempo verbal más apropiado para estas oraciones.

1. We went/have been to Mexico three times.
2. Did you go/Have you been to to Fresno by car yesterday?
3. I lived/have lived in Canada when I was a child.
4. How long are you/have you been married?
5. I met/have met Jenny's parents last Saturday.
6. Andy didn't clean/hasn't cleaned the car yet.
7. I'm sorry, but I forgot/have forgotten your wife's name. What is it?
8. The Boston train left/has left five minutes ago.

Texto en contexto

7. El festival de jazz

Complete el artículo del periódico utilizando los verbos del cuadro de la izquierda.

finish complained like received heard lived sleep written

The police have __________ over a hundred complaints about the noise from the jazz festival in City Park last weekend. "I have __________ in this street next to the park for eighteen years, and I have never __________ such a terrible noise," said Mrs. Pat Miller, of 24 Park Street. "It didn't __________ until 10:00, and our small children couldn't __________," said Mr. John Scoria, of 37 Parkside. His wife, Mrs. Jean Scoria, said, "We have __________ to the police, and we have __________ letters to the newspapers. We __________ jazz, but this music was horrible."

¡A escribir!

8. ¿Lo hizo ya?

Betty ha salido otra vez esta tarde y le ha dejado a Andy una lista de cosas que hacer en la casa. Ahora llama por teléfono para saber si todo está listo. Formule las preguntas y contéstelas, de acuerdo con la ilustración.

Ejemplo: clean up/living room *Have you cleaned up the living room yet?*
Yes, I've already cleaned it up. or: *No, I haven't cleaned it up yet.*

1. clean/car

____

2. do/shopping

____

3. cut/grass

____

4. wash/ dishes

____

5. make/sandwiches ____
6. mail/letters ____

UNIDAD 21: Old friends

En esta unidad practicaremos conversaciones con viejos amigos, mencionando eventos del pasado.

Juegos de palabras

1. Yo también

Enlace los enunciados con los comentarios correspondientes.

1. I've been traveling in Europe.
2. I crashed my car last week.
3. I'm not a teacher now
4. I'm getting married next month.
5. I haven't seen Jenny for a long time.
6. My parents have moved.
7. I was working in a shop.
8. I live in Anchorage now.
9. I wasn't earning much money.

( ) a. So have mine.
( ) b. So am I.
( ) c. So have I.
( ) d. So was I.
( ) e. Neither am I.
( ) f. Neither was I.
( ) g. So do I.
( ) h. Neither have I.
( ) i. So did I.

De persona a persona

2. ¡Hace años que no le veo!

Escriba la forma correcta del verbo en los siguientes espacios.

Jane Anne! I haven't (see) _________ you for ages! How are you?

Anne Jane, how nice to (see) _________ you. I'm fine. Hey, I (hear) _________ about your new job!

Jane Yes – I've been (work) _________ at the travel company for about two months now, and I really (like) _________ it. I haven't been in Los Angeles much, because I've been (travel) _________ in Ecuador. How about you? What have you been (do) _________ ?

Anne I'm still (work) _________ at the hospital. Hey, I (see) _________ your old boyfriend there yesterday.

Jane Who? Bob?

Anne Yes. I was (walk) _________ through the lobby, when I (see) _________ him.

Jane What was he (do) _________ there?

Anne I don't know. I was (talk) _________ to another patient at the time, so I couldn't (ask) _________ him. He was (sit) _________ in the corner, and he was (hold) _________ his head.

Jane	Oh dear. An accident?
Anne	Maybe. He was with a young woman. She (look) __________ very angry, and they weren't (talk) __________ .
Jane	Ah, a fight!

Palabras mágicas

3. Los antónimos

Escriba al frente de cada palabra su antónimo.

1. lose ______________________________
2. answer ______________________________
3. buy ______________________________
4. arrive ______________________________
5. teach ______________________________
6. receive ______________________________
7. forget ______________________________
8. wake up ______________________________

4. Sobra una

Encierre en un círculo la palabra que no pertenece al grupo.

1. cabinet newspaper sofa table chair
2. walk run swim jog hear
3. customer patient horse friend boss
4. argument talk speak tell ask
5. bring laughing crying working finding

El idioma en la mira

5. Viejos amigos

Usted acaba de encontrarse con un viejo amigo que no ha visto en años. Demuestre interés por sus comentarios haciendo preguntas con *How long ...ing?* siguiendo el ejemplo.

Ejemplo: I make clothes now.

Really? How long have you been making them?

1. I'm studying Chinese now. ______________________________
2. My sister lives in Brazil now. ______________________________

3. My brother teaches economics now. ______________________

4. Pete buys and sells cars now. ______________________

5. My mother and father both play golf now. ______________________

6. I work at the hospital now. ______________________

6. ¿Cuándo sucedió?

Ejemplo When did you meet your girlfriend? (work in El Paso)

I met her when I was working in El Paso.

1. When did you find the money? (clean the cabinet) ______________________
2. When did you break your arm? (ski in Colorado) ______________________
3. When did they get married? (live in New York) ______________________
4. When did Linda call? (talk to a customer) ______________________
5. When did he lose his wallet? (visit his parents) ______________________
6. When did you have the accident? (drive to Phoenix) ______________________

Texto en contexto

7. La carta

Ponga en orden las diferentes partes de la carta para descubrir lo que le dice Jane a su madre.

1. with his new girlfriend. They were having an argument, and his
2. time, and so I didn't buy your present - sorry. She's been
3. her yesterday! I was so surprised. I was shopping in
4. working at the hospital, and last week she saw Bob there
5. girlfriend was still hitting him there in the hospital! Ha ha ha!!
6. King Brothers Department Store for your birthday
7. Do you remember my old friend Anne? I met
8. weight, and she looks great! We were talking for a long
9. present, when I saw her. She's lost a lot of

¡A escribir!

8. ¿Qué hacía la familia cuando volvió la madre a casa?

¿Qué hacía la familia cuando volvió la madre a casa? Observe el dibujo durante un minuto, cúbralo y conteste las siguientes preguntas.

1. What was the man reading? ____________________
2. What was the man eating? ____________________
3. Was he wearing a hat? ____________________
4. What was he sitting on? ____________________
5. Where were the children playing? ____________________
6. Was the girl laughing or crying? ____________________
7. What was the boy holding? ____________________
8. Where was the cat standing? ____________________
9. What was the cat doing? ____________________

UNIDAD 22: They'll be all right.

En esta unidad practicaremos el futuro con *will* y hablaremos de la posibilidad de hacer algo.

Juegos de palabras

1. Significados semejantes

Encuentre una palabra en el segundo grupo cuyo significado sea parecido al de una palabra del primer grupo. (Tenga en cuenta que hay más palabras de las que necesita en el segundo grupo.)

hate okay fat go away probably press start speak look at

go in find also see begin weight dislike pull tell maybe right overweight talk push leave all right finish horrible

De persona a persona

2. No va a pasar nada

Phil y Betty planean una excursión para este fin de semana. Lea la conversación y luego haga preguntas que concuerden con las respuestas que se dan a continuación.

Phil I've been thinking about next weekend.

Betty Yes? What about it?

Phil Well, Friday and Monday are both holidays, aren't they?

Betty Yes ...

Phil Why don't we go away for a long weekend? Let's go to the mountains. We can go hiking.

Betty But the children hate hiking.

Phil We won't take the children. We'll leave them here.

Betty What? Leave them alone?

Phil	It's okay, nothing will happen. They'll be all right. They can take care of themselves – they're sixteen and seventeen years old now.
Betty	I know, but .... What about food?
Phil	They'll probably eat hamburgers and pizza for breakfast, lunch and dinner. Don't worry about it.
Betty	They'll probably have a party, and play loud music, and ....
Phil	No, they won't. They're sensible children.
Betty	Well, I'd like to go away for the weekend ...... Okay, let's go.

Example What has Phil been thinking about? ________ About the weekend

1. ________________ He wants to go to the mountains.
2. ________________ No, they won't take them.
3. ________________ No, they hate hiking.
4. ________________ They're 16 and 17 years old.
5. ________________ They'll probably eat hamburgers and pizza.
6. ________________ No, they won't.

Palabras mágicas

3. ¿Qué pasará?

Complete las oraciones colocando el verbo o el sustantivo apropiado.

press (x2) turn (x2)
pull lever key handle
button switch

1. What will happen if I __________ this __________ ? The window will go down.
2. What will happen if I __________ this __________ ? The lights will come on.
3. What will happen if I __________ this __________ ? The door will open.
4. What will happen if I __________ this __________ ? The engine will start.
5. What will happen if I __________ this __________ ? The radio will come on.

El idioma en la mira

4. *If* o *unless*?

Complete las frases colocando *if* o *unless* según convenga en los espacios.

Ejemplo: You'll be tired in the morning if you don't go to bed soon.

1. I won't speak to him again __________ he apologizes.
2. You'll get fat __________ you don't do more exercise.
3. You're not having any lunch __________ you don't clean up your room.
4. She won't marry him __________ he loses some weight.
5. We'll miss the train __________ we don't hurry.
6. My wife will be really angry __________ I'm late tonight.
7. You won't pass your exams __________ you study hard.
8. No thanks – I'll be sick __________ I have another beer.

5. Personalmente ...

Complete las frases con *myself, yourself, himself, herself, ourselves, yourselves* o *themselves.*

1. How did Phil learn Spanish? I think he taught __________
2. Have you ever seen __________ on video?
3. Who's crying? Have the children hurt __________ ?
4. We had a wonderful vacation – we really enjoyed __________
5. Don't worry about me – I can take care of __________
6. Who's Jane talking to? She's talking to __________ !
7. Okay everybody, let's begin the party. Please enjoy __________ !

Texto en contexto

6. Invitaciones a la fiesta

A continuación aparecen fracciones recortadas de dos invitaciones a una fiesta. ¿Puede Ud. separarlas?

1. Mom and Pop are going away for
2. It's Jane's birthday next

3. weekend (she'll be 30!) so
4. the weekend, and they'll be away until Monday, so
5. we want to have a party for her. It'll be at
6. we're going to have a party! It'll be on
7. Saturday evening, from about 8:30. I'll probably
8. my apartment on Friday evening, from about 8:00. I probably
9. cook food for the party, but could you bring
10. won't cook, because I won't have time, so could you bring
11. something to eat?
12. something to drink?
13. Thanks. See you Saturday – Linda.
14. Thanks. See you Friday – Sue.

¡A escribir!

7. ¿Estarás bien si salimos este fin de semana?

Betty está imaginándose todas las diabluras que Andy y Linda harán si ella y Phil salen este fin de semana. Construya oraciones como la que se da en el ejemplo, utilizando la información que aparece en el dibujo.

Ejemplo They'll probably have a party.

1. ______________________________

2. ______________________________

3. ______________________________

4. ______________________________

5. ______________________________

6. ______________________________

UNIDAD 23: What did you say?

En esta unidad practicaremos cómo contar lo que otras personas dijeron y la forma en que lo hicieron.

Juegos de palabras

1. ¿Cómo lo dijo?

Relacione las frases de la izquierda con el comentario apropiado.

1. We're getting married!
2. My cat died yesterday,
3. Andy! Stop that!
4. That steak looks wonderful,
5. Hush – the baby's sleeping,
6. It's 2:00 in the morning!
7. This is a very noisy party,
8. That's his new girlfriend,

( ) a. she said hungrily.
( ) b. she said quietly.
( ) c. she said loudly.
( ) d. she said sleepily.
( ) e. she said angrily.
( ) f. she said jealously.
( ) g. she said happily.
( ) h. she said sadly.

De persona a persona

2. ¿Qué dijo?

Anoche Jane recibió una llamada de Bob. Hoy ella le cuenta a su amiga, Anne, lo que él le dijo. Reconstruya el diálogo tomando cómo base el ejemplo.

Bob	I'm calling to say goodbye.
Jane	Where are you going?
Bob	(1) I'm leaving Los Angeles, and going to South America.
Jane	(2) Why are you leaving?
Bob	(3) There are too many problems for me here.
Jane	(4) What kind of problems do you have?
Bob	(5) I have all kinds of problems. (6) I don't like my job, my boss doesn't like me, and I'm having too many problems with girlfriends.
Jane	(7) What are you going to do in South America?
Bob	(8) I don't know yet. By the way, (9) what are you doing on Friday night?
Jane	(10) I'm not doing anything. (11) Why?
Bob	(12) I have two tickets to the theater.

Ejemplo: He said he was calling to say goodbye.
I asked him where he was going.

1. ______________________________
2. ______________________________
3. ______________________________
4. ______________________________
5. ______________________________
6. ______________________________
7. ______________________________
8. ______________________________
9. ______________________________
10. ______________________________
11. ______________________________
12. ______________________________

Palabras mágicas

3. Usemos los adverbios

Complete el crucigrama utilizando las pistas y descubra al final cómo regresó Bob a casa anoche.

1. Do you play the piano well? No, I play it very ________ !
2. It's ________ hot today, isn't it!
3. I ________ go to the deli for lunch, but
4. "I haven't eaten anything all day!" he said ______
5. We're late! Let's walk more ________
6. Children, you're too loud! Please play ________
7. Mom shouted at me really ________ when I broke her camera.
8. Betty plays tennis very ________
9. I'm sorry, that was too fast. Could you say it again ________

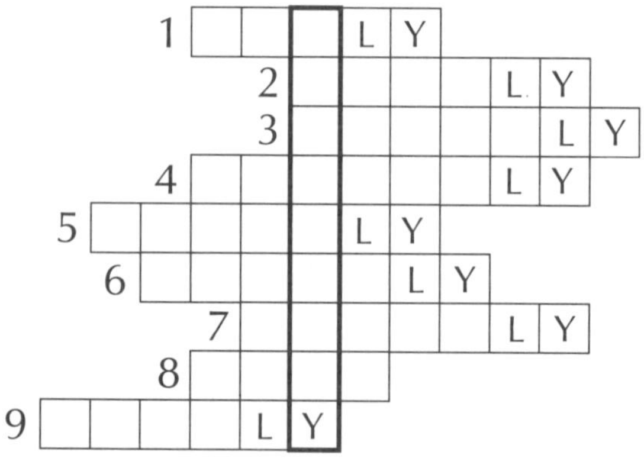

El idioma en la mira

4. Adjetivo o adverbio?

Encierre en un círculo la palabra correcta de las dos que aparecen en cada oración.

1. Do you think Anne is jealous/jealously of me?
2. Your daughter plays the piano very good/well.
3. Could you speak a little more quiet/quietly please?
4. Bob was looking very unhappy/unhappily yesterday.
5. I walked quick/quickly to the station, but I still missed the train.
6. Be careful – the cat is looking very hungry/hungrily at your fish!
7. I'm sorry I shouted at you, but I was very angry/angrily.
8. I can't hear you because the television is so loud/loudly.

5. ¿Sí o no?

Modifique estas oraciones utilizando *if*, como en el ejemplo.

Ejemplo: "Are you going home?" she asked him. **She asked him if he was going home.**

1. "Is it cold outside?" he asked her. ______________________
2. "Do you like movies?" she asked him. ______________________
3. "Do you want another coffee?" Phil asked his friend. ______________________
4. "Are you going abroad again soon?" Bob asked Jane. ______________________
5. "Are your parents well?" he asked her. ______________________
6. "Does your boyfriend play the guitar?" Jane asked Anne. ______________________

Texto en contexto

6. Lo oí en el banco

Betty estaba haciendo cola en el banco cuando oyó a dos jóvenes que tenían una conversación muy interesante detrás de ella. Después de volver a casa, se la contó a su marido, Phil. Lea lo que ella dijo y escriba de nuevo la conversación en los bocadillos que aparecen a continuación.

"He asked her what she was doing this weekend, and she said she was going to a party. So he asked her where the party was, and she told him that it was in Greenwood, and that it was going to be a very good party. He asked her why it was going to be a good party, and she said because her friend's parents were going to be away for the weekend. So he asked her what her friend's name was, and she said her friend's name was Linda, and her friend's brother's name was Andy..."

¡A escribir!

7. ¿Qué dice Ud.?

Conteste las preguntas siguiendo el ejemplo.

Ejemplo: What do you say when you want to know the price of something?

You say, "Excuse me, how much is this?"

1. What do you say when you want to know the way to the station?

2. What do you say before you go to bed at night?

3. What do you say if you want to sit next to someone on the train?

4. What do you say when you want to know what time the library closes?

5. What do you say when you want to invite someone to a movie tonight?

UNIDAD 24: Review

Esta última unidad nos permite revisar todo el trabajo hecho en las unidades anteriores.

1. Los antónimos

¿Cuál es el antónimo de cuál?

1. a little ________________________________
2. clean ________________________________
3. arrive ________________________________
4. late ________________________________
5. same ________________________________
6. always ________________________________
7. loud ________________________________
8. badly ________________________________
9. buy ________________________________
10. find ________________________________

2. Descubra las palabras

Descubra la palabra que más se adecúe a la definición.

1. _ _ rr _ _ _ _ Wear these on your ears.
2. _ _ rr _ _ The opposite of lend.
3. _ _ rr _ _ An orange vegetable.
4. _ _ rr _ _ _ _ Not nice at all.
5. _ _ rr _ Go quickly!
6. _ _ rr _ _ _ Not single.
7. _ _ rr _ You say this when you apologize.
8. _ _ _ _ rr _ _ Not today.
9. _ _ ff _ _ A hot drink.
10. _ _ ff _ _ _ _ _ Not the same.
11. _ _ ff _ _ _ _ _ Not easy.
12. _ _ gg _ You can't see well in this weather.
13. _ _ ii _ _ Do this in the snow.

3. *is/are-do/does-have/has*

Complete las frases con *is/are, do/does* o *have/has,* según corresponda.

1. _____ you mind if I don't eat all this?
2. How often _______ she call you?
3. ______ Bob have a new job in South America?
4. ______ she going to have a party on her birthday?
5. What time ________ your parent arriving?
6. I ______ never been to Panama.
7. When ______ you usually take your summer vacation?
8. Jane ______ just bought a new car.

4. Palabras que tienen el mismo sonido

Organice las palabras que suenan igual, en grupos de 3, 4 o 5.

fight height red die blue right said
late wake high why wear knew
break make night
head white straight chair weight steak bread
late wait do true care

5. Encuentre el error

Tache la palabra incorrecta de cada oración y escriba la correcta en el espacio en blanco.

1. Andy is the taller person in the family. ____________________
2. I think it's going to snowing tomorrow. ____________________
3. How about go to the theater this weekend? ____________________
4. It was Betty's birthday, because I bought her a present. ____________________
5. Would you like to go camping on August? ____________________
6. She's gone shopping, isn't she? ____________________
7. I'm not doing something tonight. ____________________
8. I've been working here since three years. ____________________

6. Crucigrama

Across

1. Can you play any ____ instruments?
4. I always ____ when I see this movie – it's so funny!
6. Jane isn't here – she's ____ shopping.
7. We're going to ____ in a hotel this year – camping is too wet!
10. It's my birthday ____ Tuesday.
11. I think it's going ____ rain.
12. I'm going to ____ an engineer when I'm older.
13. Have you ever ____ Linda's brother?
14. Bob and Anne were ____ born in Los Angeles.
17. I haven't eaten ____ today – I'm so hungry now!
18. Andy, have you ____ the grass yet?
19. I didn't go on vacation last year ____ I didn't have any money.
25. You look tired – why don't you go to bed ____ tonight?
26. It's always hot on my birthday, because it's in ____ .
27. It looks cold outside – I think it's going to ____ .
28. You ____ unhappy yesterday – were you okay?
29. I don't play tennis very well at all. In fact I play very ____ .

Down

1. We'll ____ the train if we don't run.
2. We moved to Houston three years ____ .
3. I don't have any friends in Boston – I feel so ____ .
4. ____'s go abroad this summer.
5. Ouch! My head ____ !
8. How ____ going to see a movie tonight.
9. I haven't had lunch ____ .
13. Do you ____ if I use your telephone?
15. ____ you ever been to Canada?
16. Those shoes are horrible, but ____ are nice.
20. I ____ run fast when I was younger, but I can't now.
21. I enjoyed the job, but I didn't ____ much money.
22. Please hurry – you're walking too ____ .
23. If he ____ that lever, the door will open.
24. Good – eggs and ____ again for breakfast!

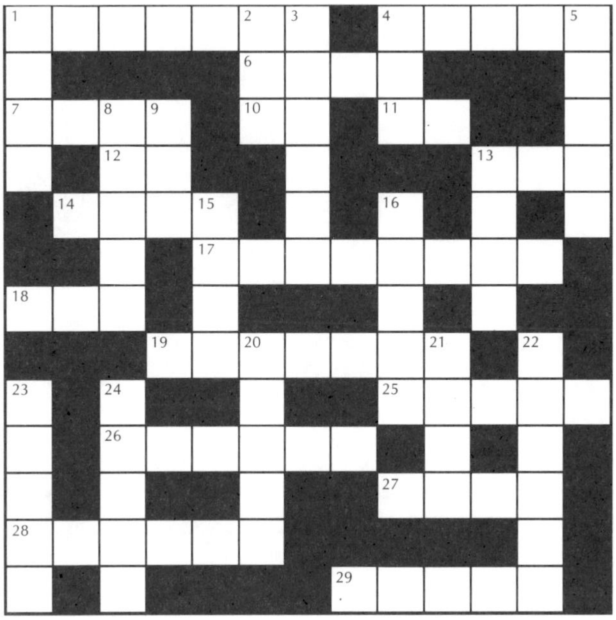

7. ¿Lo ha hecho ya?

Como Betty está hoy tan ocupada, ha hecho una lista de las cosas por hacer. A la hora del almuerzo, ¿cuáles ha hecho y cuáles le faltan?

Ejemplo: buy bread ✓ Has she bought bread yet? Yes, she has.

cut grass Has she cut the grass yet? No, she hasn't.

1. call Mom ________________
2. clean bathroom ✓ ________________
3. clean up bedrooms ✓ ________________
4. mail letters ________________
5. go to library ✓ ________________
6. take dog out ✓ ________________

8. La tarjeta postal

Las postales se escriben generalmente en forma de mensaje para ahorrar espacio. Escriba de nuevo estas frases en forma completa.

It's Tuesday today --

----

9. Preguntas personales

1. What are you wearing right now? ------------------------
2. Do you look like your mother or your father? ------------------------
3. How is the weather today? ------------------------
4. Where did you go on vacation last year? ------------------------
5. How often do you go to the dentist? ------------------------
6. Have you ever been on a diet? ------------------------
7. Where did you live when you were a child? ------------------------
8. How long have you been studying English? ------------------------

REFERENCE SECTION

Clave

UNIDAD 1

1. AM-I; IS-she, he, it, Mike; ARE-we, Mr. and Mrs. Thomas, Liz and I, they, you
2. isn't, it's, I'm, you, meet, are
3. Spain-Spanish; England-English, Bolivia-Bolivian; Cuba-Cuban; Italy-Italian; the United States-American; Canada-Canadian; Japan-Japanese; Venezuela-Venezuelan; Colombia-Colombian
4. one, two, three, four, five, six, seven, eight, nine, ten
5. 1-His name's Bob Kushner.
   2-They're from France.
   3-What's your name?
   4-I'm Betty Stones.
   5-We're American.
   6-It's coffee.
   7-She's my girlfriend.
   8-Where's my coffee?
6. 1-She isn't French.
   2-They aren't English.
   3-It isn't coffee.
   4-Her name isn't Jones.
   5-I'm not single.
7. Bob Kushner is American. He's from Los Angeles. His address is 28 River Street West. He isn't married, he's single. He's 31. His girlfriend's name is Jane. She's from Baltimore. She's 29.
8. Respuestas libres.

UNIDAD 2

1. 1-d 2-e 3-b 4-a 5-f 6-h 7-c
2. a, a, a, a, an, a, a, an, a, a, an, a, a, a
3. Jane is twenty-nine. María and Peter are thirty-two. Mary is fifty-nine. Juan is sixty-two. Alicia is eighty-one.
4. M, F, M, F, F, M, M, F, M, F, F, M, M, F 1-John 2-sister 3-husband 4-Jenny 5-son 6-niece, nephew 7-mother, father 8-grandmother
5. 1-has two 2-has one 3-has one 4-have three 5-have two 6-has three
6. 1-Do you have a car?
   2-Does John have a girlfriend?
   3-Where are Mr. and Mrs. Thomas from?
   4-What is your boss's name?
   5-How old are María's children?
   6-What is her husband's job?
7. 1-No, he hasn't. He has a new job.
   2-No, he isn't. He's a reporter now.
   3-No, it isn't. It's a big company.
   4-No, it doesn't. It has six branches.
   5-No, she isn't. She's a photographer.
8. Is your address 47 Elm Street? No, it isn't. It's 47 Oak Street. Are you married? Yes, I am. What's your husband's name? It's Phil. Is he an accountant? No, he isn't. He's a teacher. Is he from New York? No, he isn't. He's from Chicago.

UNIDAD 3

1. 1-a 2-d 3-e 4-g 5-b 6-f 7-c
2. in, are, There, Do, doors, behind, two, behind, two, near, behind
3. yellow, red, blue, orange, brown, pink, white, black, purple, green, gray
4. 1-shop 2-toilet 3-lobby 4-egg 5-gym
5. 1-some 2-a 3-any 4-a 5-any 6-some 7-any 8-an
6. 1-Is there a shower in the bathroom? Yes, there is.
   2-Is there a washing machine in the kitchen? No, there isn't.
   3-Are there any eggs in the refrigerator? Yes, there are.
   4-Are there any restaurants in Greenwood? Yes, there are.
   5-Are there any women in your office? No, there aren't.
   6-Is there a pink carpet in the living room? Yes, there is.
7. 1-swimming pool 2-gym 3-public telephones 4-coffee shop 5-bookstore 6-travel office 7-sofas, chairs and coffee tables 8-restrooms 9-French restaurant
8. 1-How many bedrooms are there?
   2-Is there a washing machine?
   3-What color is the living room?
   4-Where's the garage?
   5-Are there any trees in the yard?
   6-Where's the yard?

UNIDAD 4

1. there-chair-where eight-hate-late white-quite-right we're-near-beer new-you-do
2. 1-Andy is still in bed.
   2-Andy has got Phil's newspaper.
   3-Phil is ready.
   4-Phil likes ham and eggs.
   5- Linda doesn't like meat.
   6-Linda is a vegetarian.
3. 1-It's seven o'clock.
   2-It's half past three.
   3-It's eleven o'clock.
   4-It's half past six.

4. 1-At half past seven he's in the bath.
   2-At half past eight he's in his car.
   3-At nine o'clock he's in his office.
   4. At one o'clock he's in the coffee shop.
   5-At half past six he's in the gym.
   6-At half past eight he's in the bar.

5. 6-3-1-5-4-7-2

6. 1-it 2-them 3-her 4-him 5-me 6-it 7-us 8-it

7. 1-she is 2-she doesn't 3-you aren't 4-I do 5-I am 6-they don't

8. c-e-a-d-f-b-h-g

9. 1-Does Jenny like shopping? Yes, she does. She loves it.
   2-Do Betty and Jenny like dancing? No, they don't. They hate it.
   3-Does Jenny like golf? No, she doesn't. She doesn't like it at all.
   4-Does Pete like bars? Yes, he does. He loves them.
   5-Respuestas libres.

UNIDAD 5

1. 2-e 3-a 4-f 5-h 6-b 7-g 8-d

2. play, play, learn, learn, read, cook, watch, visit, eat, meet, meet

3. a-read b-drive c-watch d-play e-have f-write

4. Respuestas libres

5. 1-I always play football on Saturdays.
   2-Anne often visits her parents.
   3-Bob usually drives his car to work.
   4-I don't often drink red wine.
   5-Betty sometimes goes to the gym on Fridays.
   6-Linda never eats meat.

6. 1-Do, they do 2-Does, he doesn't 3-Do, I don't 4-Do, they do 5-Does, she doesn't 6-Do, I do

7. at, to, at, at, to, in, to, on, in, to, to

8. Respuestas libres

UNIDAD 6

1. 1-c 2-f 3-d 4-h 5-a 6-g 7-b 8-e

2. 1-He likes blue, gray and black.
   2-No, he doesn't.
   3-It's $99.00.
   4-She wants a cotton shirt.
   5-No, she doesn't.
   6-No, she doesn't.

3. 1-shirt 2-sweater 3-socks 4-skirt 5-tie 6-jeans 7-shoes 8-jacket 9-blouse 10-coat

4. 1-seven dollars 2-one (dollar) forty-five 3-four (dollars) ninety-nine (cents) 4-six (dollars) fifty 5-fifteen dollars 6-forty-nine (dollars)and ninety-nine cents 7-one hundred and twenty-five dollars 8-five hundred dollars

5. 1-are 2-do 3-do 4-don't 5-is 6-does 7-is 8-aren't

6. 1-How much is this watch? It's thirty-five dollars.
   2-How much are these ties? They're nine (dollars) fifty.
   3-How much is this skirt? It's twenty-four (dollars) ninety-nine.
   4-How much are these apples? They're fifty cents each.
   5-How much is this umbrella? It's seven (dollars) fifty.
   6-How much are these socks? They're two (dollars) fifty.

7. likes, hates, likes, like, goes, buys, comes, cooks, eat, eat, cook, go

8. 1-What size does she take?
   2-How much is it?
   3-What color is it?
   4-How much are they?
   5-Can I help you?
   6-Where are the ties?

UNIDAD 7

1. 1-e 2-g 3-c 4-a 5-h 6-b 7-f 8-d

2. near, see, there, over, on, your, outside, or, me, where, who

3. 1-first 2-second 3-third 4-fourth 5-fifth 6-sixth 7-seventh 8-eighth 9-ninth 10-tenth

4. 1-library 2-post office 3-swimming pool 4-bank 5-supermarket 6-butcher's 7-restaurant 8-bar

5. 1-on 2-on 3-at 4-on 5-on 6-at, on 7-on 8-at

6. 1-Excuse me, is there a telephone booth near here?
   2-The men's clothes are on the fourth floor.
   3-The bar closes at half past ten on Sundays.
   4-Turn right by the big hotel.
   5-The library is open from nine o'clock on weekdays.
   6-My house isn't far from here.

7.

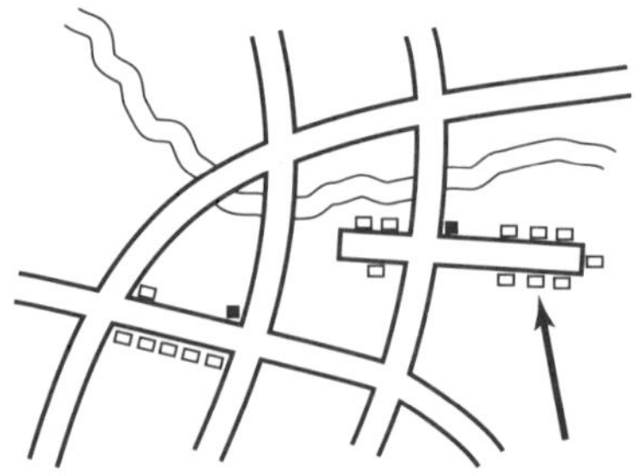

8. 1-When is the library open? It's open from ten o'clock to six o'clock on weekdays, and from ten o'clock to five o'clock on Saturdays. It's closed on Sundays.
   2-When is the post office open? It's open from nine o'clock to half past five on weekdays, and from nine o'clock to half past twelve on Saturdays. It's closed on Sundays.
   3-When is the Casa Fina restaurant open? It's open from half past six to eleven o'clock on weekdays, and from half past six to half past eleven on Saturdays. It's closed on Tuesdays and Sundays.

UNIDAD 8

1. 1-b 2-e 3-a 4-g 5-d 6-h 7-c 8-f

2. happened, had, have, saw, was, asked, told, understand, went, was, was, had, was, was, saw

3. 1-gym 2-bridge 3-go 4-tomorrow 5-white

4. 1-swimming 2-post office 3-met 4-morning 5-what

5. children, men, libraries, churches, shoes, women, families, these, people

6. 1-were 2-was 3-was 4-were 5-was 6-was

7. 1-did you go yesterday 2-did you meet her 3-did he eat 4-books did you borrow 5-did they go shopping 6-did she get up

8. 1-She saw him on Bridge Street.
2-He was with a woman.
3-Yes, they did.
4-She went home.
5-She called her mother.
6-Bob did.

9. 1-What did Jane do on Friday evening? She visited her parents.
2-What did Bob do on Saturday morning? He met Joe.
3-What did Phil do on Saturday afternoon? He went to the gym.
4-What did Anne do on Sunday evening? She went for a drink with María.
5-What did María do on Friday evening? She watched TV.

UNIDAD 9

1. 1-d 2-g 3-a 4-b 5-f 6-h 7-e 8-c

2. went, enjoyed, did you stay, was, hate, was, ate, drank, swam, danced, met, went, had, wasn't, was, went, Did you cook, cooked, ate, met

3. 1-nineteen eighty-five 2-nineteen sixty 3-eighteen eighty-one 4-nineteen ninety-four 5-seventeen hundred 6-nineteen seventy-nine 7-nineteen ninety 8-nineteen twelve

4. 1-bicycle 2-train 3-car 4-plane 5-taxi 6-motorcycle 7-subway 8-horse

5. ate, swam, drank, enjoyed, liked, stayed, wanted, see, tell, dance, meet, travel, drive, do

6. 1-No, she didn't swim in the sea every day, she swam in the pool every day.
2-No, they didn't go walking every night, they went jogging.
3-No, they didn't stay in a hotel, they stayed in a tent.
4-No, we didn't go to Costa Rica in 1989, we went to Costa Rica in 1988.
5-No, they didn't travel by car, they traveled by train.
6-No, he didn't check the oil in the car, he checked the water.

7. 1-When was she born?
2-When did the family come to the United States?
3-Where did they live?
4-Where did she go to college?
5- What did she study?
6-When did she get married?

8. 1-Did she call the camp site? Yes, she did.
2-Did she buy the food? Yes, she did.
3-Did she clean the car? No, she didn't.
4-Did she go to the bank? No, she didn't.
5-Did she clean her hiking boots? Yes, she did.
6-Did she check the tent? Yes, she did.

UNIDAD 10

1. 1-f 2-e 3-b 4-a 5-c 6-g 7-d

2. 9-3-8-2-6-1-13-7-12-5-4-13-10

3. Fruit: apple, banana, pear, lemon, orange, strawberry
Vegetables: lettuce, potato, peas, beans, carrots, onion
Meat: chicken, lamb, beef, ham, pork, sausages, steak

4. 1-half a pound of tomatoes 2-two pints of beer 3-one kilogram of apples 4-one liter of milk 5-eight ounces of ham 6-one gallon of oil

5. 1-some 2-a 3-some 4-an 5-some 6-some 7-an 8-a 9-a 10-some 11-some 12-some

6. 1-any 2-some, any 3-any 4-any 5-some, some 6-some, any

7. 1-Who had an argument yesterday? Betty and Phil did. 2-Does Phil do any exercise? No, he doesn't. 3-Does he eat a lot for breakfast? Yes, he does. 4-Who likes pizza and hamburgers? Phil does. 5-Does he often play tennis? No, he doesn't. 6-When is he fifty? Next year.

8. 1-Jane usually has some orange juice, some yogurt and some toast for breakfast. She usually has a sandwich for lunch. 2-Phil usually has some eggs, some ham, some toast and some coffee or tea for breakfast. He usually has a hamburger or a pizza for lunch. 3-Betty usually has some toast and some tea for breakfast. She usually has an apple and some cheese for lunch.

UNIDAD 11

1. 1-d 2-g 3-h 4-e 5-b 6-a 7-c 8-f

2. type, use, speak, speak, drive, drive, drive, drive, teach, love, start

3. 2-Can you paint? 3-Can you speak French? 4-Can you type? 5-Can you cook? 6-Can you drive? 7-Can you sing?

4. ACROSS: nurse, vet, policeman, waiter, reporter DOWN: actor, pilot, dentist, chef, painter, engineer, doctor

5. 1-When can I see the doctor? 2-Who can you see from the window? 3-Where can I buy some vegetables? 4-What can I cook for lunch? 5-Who can come to the party? 6-What can Betty sing?

6. 2-d 3-a 4-h 5-g 6-b 7-c 8-f

7. 1-Because she's got a new job. 2-Because she's really busy. 3-Because he wasn't at home. 4-Because it's boring. 5-Because it's fun.

8. 1-Can Phil speak Spanish? Yes, he can speak it very well. 2-Can Andy speak Spanish? No, he can't. 3-Can Betty ski? No, she can't ski very well. 4-Can Andy and Linda ski? No, they can't ski at all. 5-Can Andy play tennis? Yes, he can play it very well. 6-Can Linda speak Spanish? Yes, she can speak it a little.

UNIDAD 12

1. 1-f 2-h 3-g 4-a 5-c 6-b 7-e 8-d

2. 1-b 2-a 3-b 4-c 5-b 6-c

3. 1-first 2-four (dollars) fifty 3-sixteen 4-sixty 5-ten thousand, five hundred 6-third 7-nineteen eighty-four 8-seventy-five cents

4. 1-cold 2-never 3-good 4-white 5-open 6-easy 7-near 8-aunt 9-goodbye 10-married 11-women 12-winter

5. 1-How much are they (each)?
   2-When did you buy it?
   3-When/What time does it close?
   4-What color is it?
   5-How old is she?
   6-Do you have/Have you got any children?

6. 1-had 2-did 3-told 4-spoke 5-swam 6-came 7-went 8-met 9-drank 10-drove

7. 1-We didn't go shopping yesterday.
   2-The house doesn't have a big yard.
   3-He doesn't really like his new job.
   4-I didn't buy any fruit this morning.
   5-He doesn't get up at 7:00 every morning.
   6-They didn't go camping last year.

8. 1-What size shoes does he wear?
   2-The men's department is on the second floor.
   3-Our house is second on the right.
   4-Betty and her family stayed in a hotel.
   5-Is there any cheese in the refrigerator?
   6-I can't play tennis because I'm busy.

9. 1-close > closed 2-some > any 3-a > some 4-in > by 5-me > I 6-got > have

10. ACROSS: 1-seven 5-orange 8-weekend 10-road 11-ties 12-aunt 13-eggs 14-peas
    DOWN: 2-vegetables 3-no 4-water 6-garage 7-newspaper 8-waiter 9-dinner

UNIDAD 13

1. 1-f 2-d 3-b 4-h 5-a 6-g 7-c 8-e

2. 1-True 2-False 3-True 4-False 5-False 6-True

3. 1-happy 2-old 3-expensive 4-short 5-dark 6-short 7-small 8-light

4. 1-nose 2-mouth 3-chin 4-hair 5-eye 6-ear 7-teeth 8-neck

5. 1-shorter, shortest 2-older, oldest 3-better, best 4-longer, longest 5-happier, happiest 6-more attractive, most attractive, 7-heavier, heaviest 8-bigger, biggest 9-easier, easiest 10-slimmer, slimmest

6. 1-Mount Everest is the highest mountain in the world.
   2-Betty is more beautiful than her sister.
   3-He has longer hair than Bob.
   4-What is the longest river in the world?
   5-Andy is the tallest in his family.
   6-Was your car more expensive than mine?

7. the same, more, taller, long, eyes, wear, don't have

8. 1-Ray is the heaviest.
   2-Ray is the oldest.
   3-Enrique is the youngest.
   4-Enrique is the tallest.
   5-Enrique is younger than Sue.
   6-Ray and Sue are shorter than Enrique.
   7-Enrique and Ray have darker hair than Sue.

UNIDAD 14

1. 1-c 2-f 3-e 4-b 5-a 6-d

2. doing, calling, working, living, living, visiting, doing, washing, cleaning, working, cooking

3. 1-hot 2-working 3-now 4-week 5-umbrella 6-word processor

4. 1-living 2-writing 3-drinking 4-working 5-swimming 6-cleaning 7-singing 8-sitting 9-traveling (INDONESIA)

5. 1-take, I'm taking 2-wears, she's wearing 3-drives, is driving 4-travel, we're traveling 5-cooks, is cooking 6-go, they're going

6. 1-because 2-so 3-because 4-because 5-so 6-so

7. 1-What is she drinking?
   2-How many people are in the tour group?
   3-When did she phone Pete and Carmen?
   4-How many children do they have?
   5-Is Pete working?

8. 1-Betty isn't wearing a suit, she's wearing a dress.
   2-Jane isn't writing a postcard, she's writing a letter.
   3-Bob and his friend aren't drinking wine, they're drinking juice.
   4-Andy isn't working as a waiter, he's working as a mailman.
   5-Linda isn't skiing, she's skating.
   6-Pop isn't reading a magazine, he's reading a newspaper.

UNIDAD 15

1. 1-d 2-g 3-e 4-f 5-a 6-b 7-c

2. 1-Hold on a minute, 2-Sorry to bother you, 3-I think so. 4-We'd love to. 5-Never mind. 6-Is that okay? 7-By the way, 8-I don't know.

3. 1-3, March 2-11, November 3-4-April 4-1, January 5-12, December 6-8, August 7-2, February 8-10, October 9-9, September 10-5, May; 11-6, June; 12-7, July

4. 1-movie 2-theater 3-restaurant 4-ballet 5-party 6-disco 7-concert 8-museum

5. 1-How about seeing a movie on Wednesday?
   2-How about going for a walk this afternoon?
   3-How about playing golf on Sunday?
   4-How about going camping in August?
   5-How about staying at home this evening?
   6-How about having a party on your birthday?

6. 1-When are Bob and Jenny going to the movies?
   2-How long is Jane staying in Ecuador?
   3-What do you usually do on weekends?
   4-Does Phil always clean the car on Sundays?
   5-What are they going to see at the theater tonight?
   6-Do Betty and Phil speak French?
   7-Is Bob going to Spain in June?
   8-Is Phil coming to the ballet on Tuesday?

7. 6-8-2-7-3-5-1-9-4

8. 1-I'm sorry, but I'm visiting my mother on Tuesday evening.
   2-I'm sorry, but I'm playing golf with Tom on the afternoon of the fifth.
   3-I'm sorry, but I'm taking care of the children all day on Thursday.
   4-I'm sorry, but I'm painting the bathroom on Friday.

5-I'm sorry, but I'm taking the children to the children's theater on Saturday morning.
6-I'm sorry, but I'm going to church on Sunday morning.

UNIDAD 16

1. 1-f 2-h 3-i 4-a 5-b 6-e 7-d 8-c 9-g
2. a, a, X, the, X, X, the, the, the, the, X, a, a
3. 1-Spanish, cooking, painting, the guitar, photography, typing
   2-a soccer game, TV, movies, plays, a video,
   3-a telephone, a calendar, a camera, a computer, a clock, money
4. 1-soccer 2-guitar 3-Spanish 4-camera 5-calendar 6-clock
5. 1-aren't you? 2-don't you? 3-isn't it? 4-didn't they? 5-can't you? 6-doesn't he? 7-do you? 8-wasn't it?
6. 1-Do you mind if I listen to the radio?
   2-Do you mind if I call you at the office?
   3-Do you mind if I read your newspaper?
   4-Do you mind if I borrow your camera?
   5-Do you mind if I sit next to you?
   6-Do you mind if I close the window?
   7-Do you mind if I open the door?
7. 1-c 2-e 3-g 4-f 5-b 6-a 7-d
8.

	June			June	
M_1	TEACHING		M_8	TEACHING	
T_2	TEACHING	SWIMMING	T_9	TEACHING	SWIMMING
W_3	SPANISH		W_{10}	SPANISH	
T_4			T_{11}		
F_5	TEACHING	DANCING	F_{12}	TEACHING	SWIMMING
S_6	MOTHER		S_{13}		
S_7	COMING TO STAY		S_{14}		

9. Respuestas libres.

UNIDAD 17

1. 1-I'm going to listen to the radio.
   2-They're going to get up at 7:30.
   3-Why is he looking at me?
   4-We're going to go out tonight.
   5-I'd love to go to a movie.
   6-Can I speak to Bob, please?
   7-What are you going to write about in that letter?
2. 8-5-7-1-9-2-6-4-10-3
3. 1-listening to 2-come 3-tell 4-see 5-bring 6-understand
4. 1-Really? What kind is he going to buy?
   2-Really? What color are you going to paint it?
   3-Really? What are you going to see?
   4-Really? Where are they going to move to?
   5-Really? Who is she going to invite?
   6-Really? When are you going to start?
5. 1-anybody 2- something 3-anywhere 4-anybody
   5-somewhere 6-something 7-somebody 8-anything.
6. 1-No, there aren't. There are going to be problems with colleagues at the beginning of the month [or: There are going to be problems with money at the end of the month.]
   2-No, there isn't. There's going to be news from an old friend.
   3-No, he isn't. He's going to be jealous.
   4-No, there aren't. There are going to be arguments with my partner.
   5-No, it isn't. It's going to be a busy month socially.
   6-Yes, I am. I'm going to need a lot of exercise.
7. 1-I'm not going to learn the guitar, I'm going to learn the piano.
   2-I'm not going to become a teacher, I'm going to become an engineer.
   3-I'm not going to live in Canada, I'm going to live in Brazil.
   4-I'm not going to drive a Mercedes, I'm going to drive a Porsche.
   5-I'm not going to be beautiful, I'm going to be rich.
   6-I'm not going to have any dogs, I'm going to have some horses.

UNIDAD 18

1. 1-c 2-d 3-e 4-a 5-f 6-b
2. round-trips, returning, how much, includes, time, platform, stay, owe
3. 1-wants to 2-want to 3-want 4-want to 5-wants 6-want
   7-want to 8-want
4. 1-I'm sorry - which one?
   2-I'm sorry - to where?
   3-I'm sorry - from who(m)?
   4-I'm sorry - how much?
   5-I'm sorry - which platform?
   6-I'm sorry - how many?
   7-I'm sorry - what time/when?
   8-I'm sorry - why?
5. 1-Could you speak more slowly, please?
   2-Could I have two round-trip tickets to Chicago, please?
   3-Could you tell me the way to the station, please?
   4-Could I have some water, please?
   5-Could you stop just here, please?
   6-Could I borrow your pen, please?
6. 1-Everyone in the/our tour group was very angry.
   2-There weren't any double or twin rooms, and there weren't any showers.
   3-The rooms were dirty, and the food in the restaurant wasn't good.
   4-I/we wanted to find a different hotel, but it was too late.
   5-I had an argument with the hotel manager - he's not a very nice man!
   6-But we're all going back to the States tomorrow.
   7-Our flight arrives in L.A. at 2:30 in the afternoon.
7. (MODELOS)
   1-Could you tell me the time of the next train from New York to Providence, please? Yes, it leaves at six fifty-seven. And how long does it take? It takes two hours and twenty-six minutes.
   2-Could you tell me the time of the next train from New York to Boston, please? Yes, it leaves at eight twelve. And how long does it take? It takes three hour and forty minutes.

UNIDAD 19

1. 1-d 2-f 3-a 4-e 5-b 6-c
2. was, look, had, happened, hurts, couldn't, am meeting, took, had, was, don't want
3. 1-c-stomach 2-g-head 3-a-wrist 4-i-leg 5-f-hand 6-d-knee 7-e-ankle 8-j-foot 9-b-elbow 10-h-body
4. 1-looks like 2-look like 3-look 4-looked 5-look like
5. 1-Why don't you take an aspirin?
   2-Why don't you go to the dentist?
   3-Why don't you put on a sweater?
   4-Why don't you see a/the doctor?
   5-Why don't you go to bed early?
   6-Why don't you sit down?
   7-Why don't you go on a diet?
   8-Why don't you get more exercise?
6. 1-When I feel bored, I go to the club./I go to the club when I feel bored.
   2-Why don't you see a doctor?
   3-Bob doesn't look like his brother.
   4-I'm going to join that new sports club.
   5-You don't look very well today.
   6-I have a headache, and my feet hurt./My feet hurt, and I have a headache.
7. 1-Yes, she did. She ate lots when she was a child.
   2-No, she didn't. She didn't lose any weight when she went on a diet.
   3-No, she doesn't. She looks terrible because she can't sleep.
   4-Yes, they are. When you're overweight, diet and exercise are very important.
   5-No, you don't. You meet lots of interesting people when you do sports.
   6-No, you don't. You look better when you do exercise.
8. 1-When I went camping in Canada, it rained every day.
   2-When I was in college, I wore glasses.
   3-When I lived in San Diego, I went jogging every day.
   4-When I worked as a gardener, I was really fit.
   5-When I worked as a waiter, I got really fat.

UNIDAD 20

1. 1-e 2-f 3-g 4-a 5-c 6-h 7-b 8-d
2. 1-True 2-False 3-True 4-True 5-False 6-True
3. 1-since 2-since 3-for 4-since 5-for 6-for 7-since 8-for
4. 1-eaten Japanese food? 2-been to a pop festival? 3-ridden a horse? 4-played golf? 5-lived in an apartment? 6-drunk Australian wine? 7-broken your leg? 8-worked in a department store?
5. read, heard, seen, left, complained, taken, moved, drunk, forgotten, sung, eaten, gone, stopped, received, met, written, done
6. 1-have been 2-did you go 3-lived 4-have you been 5-met 6-hasn't cleaned 7-have forgotten 8-left
7. received, lived, heard, finish, sleep, complained, written, like
8. 1-Have you cleaned the car yet? Yes, I've already cleaned it.
   2-Have you done the shopping yet? Yes, I've already done it.
   3-Have you cut the grass yet? No, I haven't cut it yet.
   4-Have you washed the dishes yet? No, I haven't washed them yet.
   5-Have you made the sandwiches yet? Yes, I've already made them.
   6-Have you mailed the letters yet? No, I haven't mailed them yet.

UNIDAD 21

1. 1-c 2-i 3-e 4-b 5-h 6-a 7-d 8-g 9-f
2. seen, see, heard, working, like, traveling, doing, working, saw, walking, saw, doing, talking, ask, sitting, holding, looked, talking
3. 1-find 2-ask 3-sell 4-leave 5-learn/study 6-give 7-remember 8-go to bed/sleep
4. 1-newspaper 2-hear 3-horse 4-argument 5-bring
5. 1-Really? How long have you been studying it?
   2-Really? How long has she been living there?
   3-Really? How long has he been teaching it?
   4-Really? How long has he been buying and selling them?
   5-Really? How long have they been playing it?
   6-Really? How long have you been working there?
6. 1-I found it when I was cleaning the cabinet.
   2-I broke it when I was skiing in Colorado.
   3-They got married when they were living in New York.
   4-She called when I was talking to a customer.
   5-He lost it when he was visiting his parents.
   6-I had it when I was driving to Phoenix.
7. 7-3-6-9-8-2-4-1-5
8. 1-He was reading a newspaper.
   2-He was eating a hamburger.
   3-Yes, he was.
   4-He was sitting on a sofa.
   5-They were playing under the table.
   6-She was crying.
   7-He was holding a spoon.
   8-It was standing on the table.
   9-It was eating the fish.

UNIDAD 22

1. hate-dislike okay-all right fat-overweight go away-leave probably-maybe press-push start-begin speak-talk look at-see
2. 1-Where does Phil want to go?
   2-Will they take the children?
   3-Do the children like hiking?
   4-How old are the children?
   5-What will the children eat?
   6-Will they have a party?
3. 1-turn, handle 2-press, switch 3-pull, lever 4-turn,key 5-press, button
4. 1-unless 2-if 3-if 4-unless 5-if 6-if 7-unless 8-if
5. 1-himself 2-yourself 3-themselves 4-ourselves 5-myself 6-herself 7-yourselves
6. Invitation 1: 1, 4, 6, 7, 9, 12, 13 Invitation 2: 2, 3, 5, 8, 10, 11, 14
7. 1-They'll probably play loud music.
   2-They'll probably eat hamburgers for breakfast.

3-They probably won't clean up their rooms.
4-They probably won't take the dog for a walk.
5-They'll probably sleep until 12:00.
6-They'll probably watch television all day.

UNIDAD 23

1. 1-g 2-h 3-e 4-a 5-b 6-d 7-c 8-f
2. 1-He said he was leaving Los Angeles and going to South America.
   2-I asked him why he was leaving.
   3-He said there were too many problems for him here.
   4-I asked him what kind of problems he had.
   5-He said he had all kinds of problems.
   6-He said he didn't like his job, his boss didn't like him, and he was having too many problems with his girlfriends.
   7-I asked him what he was going to do in South America.
   8-He said he didn't know yet.
   9-He asked me what I was doing on Friday night.
   10-I said I wasn't doing anything.
   11-I asked him why.
   12-He said he had two tickets to the theater.
3. 1-badly 2-really 3-usually 4-hungrily 5-quickly 6-quietly 7-angrily 8-well 9-slowly (DRUNKENLY)
4. 1-jealous 2-well 3-quietly 4-unhappy 5-quickly 6-hungrily 7-angry 8-loud
5. 1-He asked her if it was cold outside.
   2-She asked him if he liked movies.
   3-Phil asked his friend if she/he wanted another coffee.
   4-Bob asked Jane if she was going abroad again soon.
   5-He asked her if her parents were well.
   6-Jane asked Anne if her boyfriend played the guitar.
6. 1-Where's the party?
   2-It's in Greenwood. It's going to be a very good party.
   3-Why is it going to be a good party?
   4-Because my friend's parents are going to be away for the weekend.
   5-What's your friend's name?
   6-My friend's name is Linda, and her brother's name is Andy.
7. 1-You say, "Excuse me, can you tell me the way to the station?"
   2-You say, "Goodnight."
   3-You say, "Excuse me, do you mind if I sit here?/next to you?"
   4-You say, "Excuse me, what time does the library close?"
   5-You say, "Would you like to see a movie tonight?"

UNIDAD 24

1. 1-a lot 2-dirty 3-leave 4-early 5-different 6-never 7-quiet 8-well 9-sell 10-lose
2. 1-earrings 2-borrow 3-carrot 4-horrible 5-hurry 6-married 7-sorry 8-tomorrow 9-coffee 10-different 11-difficult 12-foggy 13-skiing
3. 1-do 2-does 3-does 4-is 5-are 6-have 7-do 8-has
4. chair-wear-care, blue-do-knew-true, bread-said-red-head, steak-wake-break-make, wait-straight-late-great-weight, fight-white-height-right-night
5. 1-taller=tallest 2-snowing=snow 3-go=going 4-because=so 5-on=in 6-isn't=hasn't 7-something=anything 8-since=for
6. ACROSS: 1-musical 4-laugh 6-gone 7-stay 10-on 11-to 12-be 13-met 14-both 17-anything 18-cut 19-because 25-early 26-August 27-snow 28-looked 29-badly
   DOWN: 1-miss 2-ago 3-lonely 4-let 5-hurts 8-about 9-yet 13-mind 15-have 16-those 20-could 21-earn 22-slowly 23-pulls 24-bacon
7. 1-Has she called her mother yet? No, she hasn't.
   2-Has she cleaned the bathroom yet? Yes,she has.
   3-Has she cleaned up the bedrooms yet? Yes, she has.
   4-Has she mailed the letters yet? No, she hasn't.
   5-Has she been to the library yet? Yes, she has.
   6-Has she taken the dog out yet? Yes, she has.
8. It's Tuesday today. It has been very hot every day, but it's raining today. The hotel is great - it's very small and quiet, but it has a big swimming pool, and two restaurants. There are lots of interesting people. We've been swimming every day. Shopping is difficult, because we don't speak the language! But the local people are very nice, and the food is wonderful. We'll be home/We're coming home on Saturday, so we'll see you then.
9. (respuestas possibles)
   1-I'm wearing (jeans).
   2-I look like my (father).
   3-It's (raining).
   4-I went to (Spain).
   5-I go to the dentist (twice a year).
   6-Yes, I have/No, I haven't.
   7-I lived in (California).
   8-I've been studying English (for three years).

Gramática

VERBOS REGULARES en este texto

INFINITIVO	PASADO SIMPLE/PARTICIPIO PASADO	INFINITIVO	PASADO SIMPLE/PARTICIPIO PASADO
answer	answered	miss	missed
apologize	apologized	move	moved
arrive	arrived	need	needed
ask	asked	open	opened
believe	believed	order	ordered
borrow	borrowed	owe	owed
call	called	paint	painted
carry	carried	pass	passed
cause	caused	phone	phoned
check	checked	play	played
clean	cleaned	post	posted
close	closed	press	pressed
complain	complained	pull	pulled
cook	cooked	receive	received
crash	crashed	remember	remembered
cry	cried	reserve	reserved
dance	danced	return	returned
die	died	shout	shouted
dislike	disliked	start	started
earn	earned	stay	stayed
enjoy	enjoyed	stop	stopped
finish	finished	study	studied
happen	happened	talk	talked
hate	hated	tidy	tidied
help	helped	travel	traveled
hurry	hurried	turn	turned
include	included	type	typed
invite	invited	use	used
join	joined	visit	visited
laugh	laughed	want	wanted
live	lived	watch	watched
look	looked	whisper	whispered
marry	married	work	worked
mind	minded	worry	worried

VERBOS IRREGULARES en este texto

INFINITIVO	PASADO SIMPLE	PARTICIPIO PASADO	INFINITIVO	PASADO SIMPLE	PARTICIPIO PASADO
be	was/were	been	learn	learnt/learned	learnt/learned
become	became	become	leave	left	left
begin	began	begun	lose	lost	lost
break	broke	broken	make	made	made
bring	brought	brought	meet	met	met
buy	bought	bought	pay	paid	paid
can	could	been able	read	read	read
come	came	come	ride	rode	ridden
cut	cut	cut	say	said	said
do	did	done	see	saw	seen
drink	drank	drunk	sell	sold	sold
eat	ate	eaten	shine	shone	shone
fall	fell	fallen	sing	sang	sung
feel	felt	felt	sit	sat	sat
find	found	found	sleep	slept	slept
forget	forgot	forgotten	speak	spoke	spoken
get	got	gotten	swim	swam	swum
give	gave	given	take	took	taken
go	went	gone/been	teach	taught	taught
have	had	had	tell	told	told
hear	heard	heard	think	thought	thought
hit	hit	hit	understand	understood	understood
hold	held	held	wear	wore	worn
hurt	hurt	hurt	write	wrote	written
know	knew	known			

Ejemplos de cómo utilizar los diferentes tiempos:

Presente simple:

you play	you don't play	do you play?
he plays	he doesn't play	does he play?

Pasado simple:

you played	you didn't play	did you play?
he played	he didn't play	did he play?

Presente continuo:

you are (you're) playing	you aren't playing	are you playing?
he is (he's) playing	he isn't playing	is he playing?

Pasado continuo:

you were playing	you weren't playing	were you playing?
he was playing	he wasn't playing	was he playing?

Presente perfecto:

you have (you've) played he has (he's) played	you haven't played he hasn't played	have you played? has he played?

Presente perfecto continuo:

you have (you've) been playing he has (he's) been playing	you haven't been playing he hasn't been playing	have you been playing? has he been playing?

COMPARATIVOS Y SUPERLATIVOS

ADJETIVO	COMPARATIVO	SUPERLATIVO
cheap	cheaper	cheapest
old	older	oldest
fast	faster	fastest
tall	taller	tallest
angry	angrier	angriest
busy	busier	busiest
dirty	dirtier	dirtiest
easy	easier	easiest
hot	hotter	hottest
big	bigger	biggest
expensive	more expensive	most expensive
handsome	more handsome	most handsome
interesting	more interesting	most interesting
beautiful	more beautiful	most beautiful
good	better	best
bad	worse	worst

Ejemplos:

Jane is taller than her brother.
I think Betty is much more beautiful than Jane.
This is the biggest room in the house.
I bought the most expensive shoes in the store.

PRONOMBRES PERSONALES

PRONOMBRE SUJETO	PRONOMBRE OBJETO	ADJETIVO POSESIVO
I	me	my
you	you	your
she	her	her
he	him	his
it	it	its
we	us	our
you	you	you
they	them	their

Ejemplos:

I don't like her very much. She always shouts at me.
They invited us to their party.
We told him about our vacation.

NÚMEROS

1 one	11 eleven	21 twenty-one	40 forty
2 two	12 twelve	22 twenty-two	50 fifty
3 three	13 thirteen	23 twenty-three	60 sixty
4 four	14 fourteen	24 twenty-four	70 seventy
5 five	15 fifteen	25 twenty-five	80 eighty
6 six	16 sixteen	26 twenty-six	90 ninety
7 seven	17 seventeen	27 twenty-seven	100 a hundred
8 eight	18 eighteen	28 twenty-eight	1,000 a thousand
9 nine	19 nineteen	29 twenty-nine	1,000,000 a million
10 ten	20 twenty	30 thirty	

Cómo decir los números:

397	three hundred and ninety-seven
4,850	four thousand, eight hundred and fifty
50,000	fifty thousand
650,000	six hundred and fifty thousand
1,400,000	one million, four hundred thousand

PRECIOS

Cómo decir los precios:

50¢	fifty cents
75¢	seventy-five cents
$1.00	a dollar
$1.20	a dollar twenty
$8.50	eight dollars fifty cents
$250.00	two hundred and fifty dollars

MESES

January	April	July	October
February	May	August	November
March	June	September	December

DÍAS DE LA SEMANA

Monday	Friday
Tuesday	Saturday
Wednesday	Sunday
Thursday	

FECHAS

1st first	11th eleventh	21st twenty-first
2nd second	12th twelfth	22nd twenty-second
3rd third	13th thirteenth	23rd twenty-third
4th fourth	14th fourteenth	24th twenty-fourth
5th fifth	15th fifteenth	25th twenty-fifth
6th sixth	16th sixteenth	26th twenty-sixth
7th seventh	17th seventeenth	27th twenty-seventh
8th eighth	18th eighteenth	28th twenty-eighth
9th ninth	19th nineteenth	29th twenty-ninth
10th tenth	20th twentieth	30th thirtieth
		31st thirty-first

Cómo decir las fechas:

Jan 3, 1994 January the third, nineteen ninety-four
Aug 9, 1949 August the ninth, nineteen forty-nine
1/5/91 January the fifth, nineteen ninety-one

LA HORA

Cómo decir la hora:

10:00 ten o'clock
11:30 half past eleven, or eleven thirty
2:15 quarter past two, or two fifteen
3:45 quarter to four, or three forty-five
4:10 ten past four, or four ten
5:40 twenty to six, or five forty
7:00 a.m. seven o'clock in the morning
3:00 p.m. three o'clock in the afternoon
8:00 p.m. eight o'clock in the evening

ABREVIATURAS

a.m.	before noon (ante meridiem)	gm	gram	ft	foot
		lb	pound	in	inch
p.m.	after noon (post meridiem)	oz	ounce	US	the United States
$	dollar	cm	centimeter	USA	the United States of America
¢	cent	m	meter	UK	United Kingdom
kg	kilogram	km	kilometer	GB	Great Britain

VOCABULARIO

El número que aparece después de cada palabra indica el número de la unidad en que ésta aparece por primera vez.

A

a little	un poco 11
a lot of	mucho [de] 9
a/an	un/uno 2
about	más o menos/sobre 6
accident	accidente 21
accountant	contador 2
actor	actor 11
address	dirección 1
after	después 5
afternoon	(la) tarde 15
age	edad 1
agenda	agenda 15
ago…	hace… 20
airport	aeropuerto 18
all right	está bien 22
all	todo 9
alone	solo 22
along (the street)	a lo largo de… 7
already	ya 20
also	también 9
always	siempre 5
an	un/uno 2
and	y 1
angrily	airadamente 23
angry	enojado 8
ankle	tobillo 19
another	otro 8
answer (v)	contestar 21
any	algún/(negativo: ningún) 3
anybody	cualquiera/(negativo: nadie) 17
anything	cualquier cosa 8
anywhere	cualquier parte 17
apartment	apartamento 14
apologize (v)	disculparse 22
apple	manzana 3
April	abril 15
argument	riña, discusión 8
arm	brazo 21
arrive (v)	llegar 18
art gallery	galería de arte 7
artist	pintor 11
as/as in	como/en 2
ask (v)	pedir 8
aspirin	aspirina 19
at	a 4
at the end	al final 7
attractive	atractivo 9
August	agosto 15
aunt	tía 2
awful	terrible 19

B

back	de vuelta 18
bacon	tocino 24
bad	mal/o 2
badly	mal 23
bag	bolsa 6
ballet	ballet 15
banana	plátano 10
bank	banco 7
bar	bar 4
barbecue	parrillada 15
bath	baño 3
bathroom	cuarto de baño 3
be (v)	ser/estar 1
be careful	¡ten cuidado! 17
beans	alubias 10
beautiful	hermoso 13
because	porque 11
become (v)	pasar a ser 17
bed	cama 4
bedroom	cuarto/recámara 3
beef	carne de vaca 10
beer	cerveza 4
begin (v)	empezar 22
beginning	principio 17
behind	detrás de 3
believe (v)	creer 9
between	entre 3
bicycle	bicicleta 9
big	grande 2
birthday	cumpleaños 14
bit	trozo/poco 8
black	negro 3
blouse	blusa 6
blue	azul 3
body	cuerpo 19
Bolivia/Bolivian	Bolivia/boliviano 1
book	libro 3
bookstore	librería 3
booth	cabína 7
boots	botas 9
bored	aburrido 19
boring	aburrido 11

born	nació 9
borrow (v)	pedir prestado 7
boss	jefe 2
both	ambos 14
boyfriend	novio 5
branch	sucursal 2
bread	pan 10
break (v)	romper 17
breakfast	desayuno 4
bridge	puente 7
bring (v)	traer 15
brochure	folleto 9
brother	hermano 2
brown	café/marrón 3
building	edificio 3
bus	camión/autobús 9
busy	ocupado 5
but	pero 3
butcher	carnicero 7
button	botón 22
buy (v)	comprar 6
by	por/en 9
by the way	a propósito 7

C

cabinet	armario 21
cake	torta/pastel 19
calendar	calendario 16
call (v)	llamar 8
camera	cámara fotográfica 15
camping site	campamento 9
camping	acampar 9
Can I help you?	¿Lo puedo ayudar? 6
can (v)	poder 11
Canada/Canadian	Canada/canadiense 1
car	carro 2
carpet	alfombra 3
carrots	zanahorias 10
carry (v)	llevar 14
casual	de sport 6
cat	gato 3
cause (v)	causar 17
cent	centavo 6
centimeter (cm.)	centímetro 13
chair	silla 3
change (v)	cambiar 16
cheap	barato 6
check (v)	controlar 9
cheese	queso 10
chef	cocinero 11
chicken	pollo 10
child/children	niño/a/niños/as 2
chin	quijada 13
church	iglesia 7
class	clase 16
clean (v)	limpiar 9
clean up (v)	ordenar/acomodar 20
clock	reloj 16
close (v)	cerrar 7
closed	cerrado 7
clothes	ropa 14
club	club 16
coat	chaqueta 6
coffee	café 1
coffee shop	café (cafetería) 3
cold (n)	catarro 20
cold	frío 9
colleague	colega 17
college	universidad 9
Colombia/Colombian	Colombia/colombiano 1
color	color 6
come (v)	venir 5
come on (v) (lights)	prenderse (de luces) 22
company	compañía 2
complain (v)	quejarse 20
complaint	queja 20
computer	computadora 3
concert	concierto 15
cook (n)	cocinero 19
cook (v)	cocinar 5
cooking (n)	(la) cocina 6
corner	rincón 3
cotton	algodón 6
Could I/you ...?	¿Podría.../Ud? 18
country/countries	país/países 1
crash (v)	estrellar 17
credit card	tarjeta de crédito 18
crossroads	cruce 7
cry (v) 21	llorar
Cuba/Cuban	Cuba/cubano 1
cup	taza 10
customer	cliente 18
cut (v)	cortar 20

D

dance (v)	bailar 9
dancing	bailando 4
dark	oscuro 13
date (appointment)	cita 8
date (day/month)	fecha 15
daughter	hija 2
day	día 14
December	diciembre 15
dentist	dentista 11
department	departamento 7
desk	escritorio 3
dessert	postre 19
die (v)	morir 23
diet	régimen 17
different	diferente16
difficult	difícil 5
dinner	cena 5
dirty	sucio 18
disco	disco 9
dislike (v)	tener aversión a 22
do (v)	hacer 5

do you ever ...?	¿alguna vez...? 16
do you mind if ...?	¿le importa si...? 16
dog	perro 15
dollar	dólar 6
don't worry	no se preocupe 11
door	puerta 3
down	abajo 22
dress	vestido (de mujer) 14
drink (v)	beber 5
driver	conductor 11
drunk	borracho 13
drunkenly	como borracho 23

E

each	cada (uno) 6
early	temprano 19
earn (v)	ganar 21
earrings	pendientes 13
ears	orejas 13
easy	fácil 6
eat (v)	comer 5
eat out (v)	comer afuera 9
economics	ciencias económicas 9
egg	huevo 3
eight	ocho 1
eighth	octavo 7
elbow	codo 19
end	final 17
engine	motor 22
engineer	ingeniero 2
England/English	Inglaterra/inglés 1
enjoy (v)	disfrutar de 9
Europe	Europa 9
evening	noche 5
ever (did you...?)	(¿alguna vez...?) 20
every	cada 9
exam	examen 17
example	ejemplo 1
excuse me	con permiso 2
exercise	ejercicio 10
expensive	caro 6
extra	extra 19

F

fair	rubio 13
fall (v)	caer 17
false	falso 13
family	familia 5
far	lejos 7
fast	rápido 23
fat	gordo 10
father	padre 2
February	febrero 15
feel (v)	sentir 19
festival	festival 20
fifth	quinto 7
fight	pelea 21
find (v)	encontrar 21
fine	bueno/de acuerdo 15
finish (v)	terminar 5
first name	nombre de pila 2
first	primero 7
fish	pescado 6
five	cinco 1
flight	vuelo 18
floor	piso 7
flu	gripe 19
fog	bruma 14
foggy	nebuloso 14
food	comida 5
foot	pie 19
for (period of time)	para 20
for ages	por mucho tiempo 21
for	para 6
foreign	extranjero 11
forget (v)	olvidar 20
four	cuatro 1
fourth	cuarto 7
France/French	Francia/francés 1
free	libre 5
free time	tiempo libre 16
French fries	papas fritas 10
Friday	viernes 5
friend	amigo 5
from	de 1
fruit	fruta 10
fun	diversión 9
funny	gracioso 23
future	futuro 17

G

gallon (gal.)	galón 10
game	juego 16
garage	garaje 3
gardener	jardinero 19
German	alemán 11
get (v)	obtener 17
get married (v)	casarse 9
get up (v)	levantarse 5
girlfriend	novia 1
give (v)	dar 15
glass	vidrio 10
glasses	lentes 13
gloves	guantes 6
go (v)	ir 5
go ahead (v)	adelantar(se) 16
go away	irse 22
go camping (v)	ir a campar 9
go for a walk (v)	dar un paseo 15
go shopping (v)	ir de compras 8
go skiing (v)	ir a esquiar 9
go to bed (v)	acostarse 5
golf	golf 4
good	bueno 2
good idea	buena idea 6
good luck	buena suerte 19

good morning	buenos días 1
goodbye	adiós 2
grandchild	nieto 2
grandfather	abuelo 2
grandmother	abuela 2
grass	pasto 20
gray	gris 6
great (we had a ...)	lo pasamos muy bien 9
great time	pasarlo bien? 9
green	verde 3
guide	guía 11
guitar	guitarra 5
gym	gimnasio 3

H

hair	pelo 13
half past... (time)	...y media (hora) 4
ham	jamón 10
hamburger	hamburguesa 10
hand	mano 19
handle	mango 22
handsome	guapo 13
hangover	resaca 19
happen (v)	pasar 8
happily	por fortuna 23
happy	feliz 13
hard	duro 22
has/have got	tiene/tienen 2
hat	sombrero 14
hate (v)	odiar 4
have (v)	tener 6
have a drink (v)	tomar algo 7
have a shower/bath (v)	regaderarse/bañarse 5
have lunch (v)	comer/almorzar 5
have you ever ...?	¿Alguna vez ...? 20
he	el 1
head	cabeza 19
headache	dolor de cabeza 19
health	salud 17
healthy	saludable 17
hear (from) (v)	recibir noticias de 17
hear (v)	oir/escuchar 20
hear about (v)	recibir información sobre 21
heavy	pesado 13
height	estatura/talla 13
hello	hola 2
help (v)	ayudar 19
her	su 1
here	aquí 4
here it is	aquí está 6
herself	ella misma 22
hey!	¡oye! 7
hi	hola 2
high	alto 13
hiking	excursionismo a pie 9
him	el 4
himself	el mismo 22
his	su 1
hit (v)	golpear 21
Hold on a minute.	Un momentito. 15
hold (v)	tener 21
home	casa 5
horrible	horrible 10
horse	caballo 9
hospital	hospital 21
hot	caliente 9
hotel	hotel 3
hour	hora 18
house	casa 3
How about ...?	¿Y que le parece si...? 5
How about ...ing?	¿Que tal si...? 15
How are you?	¿Cómo le va? 2
How do you do?	Mucho gusto. 1
how long?	¿cuánto tiempo? 21
how many?	¿cuántos? 3
how much?	¿cuánto? 6
How nice to see you.	Que gusto verle/los. 21
how old?	¿cuántos años? 2
hungrily	ansiosamente 23
hungry	hambriento 10
hurry (v)	apurarse 22
hurt (v)	dañar 19
husband	marido/esposo 2

I

I don't believe you.	No le creo. 9
I don't care.	No me importa. 20
I see.	Entiendo. 2
I think so.	Creo que sí. 15
I'd like...	Me gustaría... 10
I'd/we'd love to.	Me/nos encantaría. 15
I'm fine	Me siento muy bien. 2
I'm sorry	Lo siento 1
if	si 22
important	importante 11
in	en/dentro (de) 3
in fact	en realidad 4
in front of	por delante de 15
include (v)	incluir 18
India	India 9
inside	(a)dentro 7
interesting	interesante 5
international	internacional 2
into	en/dentro de/a 6
invitations	invitaciones 17
invite (v)	invitar 15
Ireland	Irlanda 9
it doesn't matter	no importa 17
it	lo 1
Italy/Italian	Italia/italiano 1

J

jacket	chaqueta 6
January	enero 15
Japan/Japanese	Japón/japonés 1
jazz	jazz 20

jealous	celoso 17
jealously	celosamente 23
jeans	blue jeans 6
job	trabajo 2
jogging	jogging 8
join (v)	asociarse/ingresar a 19
July	julio 15
June	junio 15
just a minute	momentito 16
just	solo/solamente 8

K

key	llave 22
kilogram (kg)	kilogramo 10
kitchen	cocina 3
knee	rodilla 19
knife	cuchillo 3
know (v)	saber/conocer 6

L

label	etiqueta 6
lamb	cordero 10
language	lenguaje 11
large	grande 6
last night	anoche 11
last week	la semana pasada 10
last year	el año pasado 9
late	tarde 4
later	más tarde 19
laugh (v)	reír(se) 21
learn (v)	aprender 5
leather	cuero 13
leave (v)	partir/dejar 18
left	izquierda 3
leg	pierna 19
lemon	limón 10
lesson	clase 16
let's see	vamos a ver 16
letter	carta 5
lettuce	lechuga 10
lever	palanca 22
library	biblioteca 7
life	vida 5
light (n)	luz 22
light	ligero/de poco peso 13
like (v)	gustar 4
listen to (v)	escuchar 16
liter	litro 10
little	poco 10
live (v)	vivir 5
living room	sala de estar 3
lobby	antesala 3
lonely	solo 19
long	largo 13
look (appearance) (v)	parecer 19
look (v)	mirar 8
look at (v)	mirar algo 16
look forward to (v)	tener ganas de 15
look like (v)	parecerse 13
lose (v)	perder 19
lots of	mucho/a/s 11
loud	ruidoso 23
love	querer 4
lunch	almuerzo 10
lunchtime	hora de almuerzo 20

M

magazine	revista 14
mail (v)	enviar por correo 17
mailman	cartero 14
make (v)	hacer 11
manager	gerente 18
March	marzo 15
married	casado 1
marry (v)	casarse 22
May	mayo 15
maybe	quizá 6
me	yo 4
meat	carne 4
medium	medio 6
meet (v)	encontrar(se) 5
meeting	reunión 15
men	hombres 7
milk	leche 10
mind (v)	importar 16
minute	minuto 16
miss (v)	extrañar 22
mistake	error 2
mom	mamá 4
Monday	lunes 5
money	dinero 7
month	mes 16
more	más 10
morning	mañana 4
mother	madre 2
motorcycle	motocicleta 9
mountain	montaña 13
mouth	boca 13
move (house)	cambiar de casa 20
move (v)	mover 9
movie/s	película/s 15
movie house	cine 15
Mr.	Sr 1
Ms.	Sra/Srta 1
museum	museo 15
music	música 20
musical instrument	instrumento musical 16
my	mi 1
myself	yo mismo/a 22

N

name	nombre 1
nationality	nacionalidad 1
near	cerca 3
nearly	casi 20
neck	cuello 13

need (v)	necesitar 17
neither	ni 21
nephew	sobrino 2
Never mind!	¡No se preocupe! 15
never	nunca 5
new	nuevo 2
news	noticias 2
newspaper	periódico 5
next to	al lado de 3
next year	el año que viene 10
nice	agradable 2
niece	sobrina 2
night	noche 8
nine	nueve 1
ninth	noveno 7
no	no 1
no, thank you	no gracias 4
noise	ruido 20
nose	nariz 13
not any more	no...más/ahora 19
not at all	en absoluto 4
nothing	nada 16
November	noviembre 15
now	ahora 2
numbers	números 1
nurse	enfermera 11

O

o'clock	son las... 4
October	octubre 15
odd	raro/extraño 14
of course	por supuesto 16
office	oficina 2
often	muchas veces 5
oh dear	¡Ay que lástima! 21
oil	aceite 9
okay (=OK)	¡está bien! 2
old	viejo 13
omelet	tortilla 10
on	sobre 3
on the phone	por teléfono 15
one (n)	un(o) 6
one	uno 1
onion	cebolla 10
only	solo 8
open (v)	abrir 10
open	abierto 7
opera	ópera 11
opposite	enfrente de 7
or	o 3
orange	naranja 3
order (v)	ordenar 10
ounce (oz.)	onza 10
our	nuestro 4
ourselves	nosotros mismos 22
outside	fuera 7
over	encima 7
over there	allá 16
overseas	en el extranjero 16
overweight	demasiado pesado 19
owe (v)	deber 18

P

pain	dolor 19
paint (v)	pintar 11
painter	pintor 11
parents	padres 5
park	parque 3
part-time	de medio tiempo 16
partner	socio 17
party	fiesta 11
pass an exam (v)	aprobar un examen 17
patient	paciente 21
pay (v)	pagar 18
pear	pera 10
peas	chícharos 10
pen	pluma 18
people	gente 3
person	persona 8
phone (v)	llamar (por teléfono) 14
photograph	fotografía 13
photographer	fotógrafo 2
photography	fotografía 16
pianist	pianista 11
piano	piano 11
pilot	piloto 11
pink	rosado 3
pint (pt)	pinta 10
pizza	pizza 10
plane	avión 9
platform	plataforma 18
play (v)	jugar 5
play	obra de teatro 16
please	por favor 1
pleased to meet you	encantado de conocerlo 1
poetry	poesía 5
police	policía 20
policeman	policía 2
pop	música pop 20
pop	papá 4
popular	popular 6
pork	carne de cerdo 10
post office	casa de correos 7
postcard	tarjeta postal 14
potato	papa 10
pound (lb.)	libra 10
present	regalo 6
press (v)	apretar 22
pretty	bonito 8
price	precio 6
probably	probablemente 20
problem	problema 8
pub	bar (inglés) 12
public	público 3
pull (v)	tirar 22
purple	morado 3

Q

quarter	cuarto 5
quarter past	...y cuarto 5
quarter to	...menos cuarto 5
questions	preguntas 11
quickly	rápidamente 18
quiet	silencioso 14
quietly	silenciosamente 23

R

radio	radio 16
rain	lluvia 14
raining	lloviendo 14
read (v)	leer 5
ready	listo 4
really	realmente 8
really?	¿de veras? 9
receive (v)	recibir 20
red	rojo 3
refrigerator	refrigerador 3
remember (v)	recordar 14
reporter	periodista 2
reservations	reservas 18
restaurant	restaurante 3
restroom	servicios 3
return (v)	volver 18
rich	rico 17
ride (v)	ir (en bicicleta) 11
right	derecha 3
right now	ahora mismo 14
river	río 7
road	calle 7
room	cuarto 17
round-trip ticket	boleto de ida y vuelta 18
run (v)	correr 21

S

sad	triste 13
sadly	tristemente 23
salad	ensalada 10
same as	lo mismo que 13
same	mismo 5
sandwich	sándwich 3
Saturday	sábado 5
sauna	sauna 3
sausage	salchicha 10
say (v)	decir 23
scarf	bufanda 14
sea	mar 9
second	segundo 7
secretary	secretaria 11
see (v)	ver 8
sell (v)	vender 21
sensible	sensato 22
September	septiembre 15
seven	siete 1
seventh	séptimo 7
she	ella 1
shine (v)	brillar 14
shirt	camisa 6
shoes	zapatos 6
shop	tienda 3
shopping	las compras 4
short	corto 13
shout (v)	gritar 23
shower	regadera 3
sick	enfermo 15
sightseeing	turismo 9
sign	señal 7
silk	seda 6
sing (v)	cantar 11
singer	cantante 11
single	solo 1
sink	fregadero/pileta 3
sister	hermana 2
sit (v)	sentarse 14
six	seis 1
sixth	sexto 7
size	tamaño 6
skating	patinaje 14
skiing	esquí 9
skimmed	desnatado 10
skirt	falda 6
sleep (n)	sueño 17
sleep (v)	dormir 14
sleepily	soñolientamente 23
slim	delgado 13
slowly	lentamente 23
small	pequeño 2
snow	nieve 14
snowing	nevando 14
so	entonces 14
so many	tantos 20
soap	jabón 3
soccer	fútbol l5
socially	socialmente 17
socks	calcetines 6
sofa	sofá 3
some	algunos 3
somebody	alguien 16
something	algo 17
sometimes	algunas veces 5
somewhere	en alguna parte 17
son	hijo 2
song	canción 11
Sorry to bother you.	Perdone la molestia. 15
sorry	perdón 1
soup	sopa 10
Spain/Spanish	España/español 1
speak (v)	hablar 11
spoon	cuchara 21
sports center	centro deportivo 18
sports	deportes 3
stamps	timbres/sellos 7
start (v)	empezar 5
States (the...)	los Estados Unidos 14

station	estación 15
stay (v)	quedar(se) 9
stay up (v)	mantenerse de pie 22
steak	bistec 10
still	todavía? 4
stomach	estómago 19
stop (v)	parar 20
store	tienda 3
story	historia 8
straight ahead	derecho 7
straight on	derecho 7
strange	extraño 5
strawberry	fresa 10
street	calle 7
strong	fuerte 13
student	estudiante 9
study (v)	estudiar 9
subway	(tren) subterráneo 9
suit	traje 14
summer	verano 9
sun	sol 14
Sunday	domingo 5
supermarket	supermercado 6
surprised	sorprendido 8
sweater	suéter 6
swim (v)	nadar 7
swimming	natación 4
swimming pool	piscina 3
switch	llave 22

T

table	mesa 3
take (a size) (v)	medir 6
take (time) (v)	ir despacio 18
take (v)	tomar 15
take care (v)	tener cuidado 14
talk (v)	hablar 21
tall	alto 13
taxi driver	taxista 18
taxi	taxi 9
tea	té 1
teach (v)	enseñar 11
teacher	profesor 2
teeth	dientes 13
telephone booth	cabina telefónica 7
telephone call	llamada telefónica 17
telephone	teléfono 3
television	televisión 3
tell (v)	contar 8
ten	diez 1
tennis	tenis 5
tent	tienda de campaña 9
tenth	décimo 7
terrible	terrible 18
thank you	gracias 1
that	aquel 5
that's right	eso es 13
the	el 3
theater	teatro/cine 15
their	su 4
them	ellos 4
themselves	ellos mismos 22
then	entonces 7
there	allí 7
there is/are	hay 3
these	estos 6
they	ellos 1
thing	cosa 15
think (v)	pensar 23
third	tercero 7
thirsty	sediento 19
this	este/a 4
this/that way	por aquí/por allá 7
those	ésos 9
three	tres 1
Thursday	jueves 5
ticket	boleto 16
tie	corbata 6
time	tiempo 4
tired	cansado/a 19
to	a 5
today	hoy 14
toilet	servicios 3
tomato	tomate 10
tomorrow	mañana 5
tonight	esta noche 14
too much	demasiado 19
too	también 3
toothache	dolor de muelas 19
tour group	grupo de turistas 18
tour guide	guía de turistas 11
tourist	turista 7
train	tren 9
travel (n)	viaje 2
travel (v)	viajar 9
travelers' checks	cheques de viajero 18
traveling	viajando 9
trip	viaje 19
true	verdad 13
Tuesday	martes 5
turn (v)	girar 7
two	dos 1
type (v)	escribir a máquina 11
typing	escribiendo a máquina 16

U

umbrella	paraguas 3
uncle	tío 2
under	abajo de 3
understand (v)	comprender 7
unfit	no en forma 19
unhappy	infeliz 23
United States	Estados Unidos 1
unless	a menos que 22
until	hasta 7
us	nosotros 4

use (v)	usar 11
usually	normalmente 5

V

vacation	vacación 9
vegetables	verduras 10
vegetarian	vegetariano 4
Venezuela/n	Venezuela/venezolano 1
very much	mucho 4
very	muy 2
vet	veterinario 11
video	video 16
visit (v)	visitar 5

W

waiter	mesero 11
walk (n)	paseo 20
wallet	billetera 21
want (v)	querer 6
want to (v)	querer 18
wash (v)	lavar 14
washing machine	lavadora 3
watch (n)	reloj 6
watch (v)	mirar 5
water	agua 9
we	nosotros 1
wear (v)	llevar 6
weather	tiempo 11
Wednesday	miércoles 5
week	semana 10
weekday	día de semana 7
weekend	fin de semana 5
weight	peso 13
Welcome back!	¡Bienvenido nuevamente! 19
well	bien 8; sano 11
wet	mojado 9
what kind?	¿de qué tipo? 17
what time?	¿a qué hora? 4
What's happening/on?	¿qué dan (cine)? 15
what?	¿qué? 4
when I was ...	cuando yo era... 19
when?	¿cuándo? 8
where?	¿dónde? 1
which?	¿cuál? 7
whiskey	whisky 16
whisper (v)	chuchichear 23
white	blanco 3
who?	¿quién? 4
Why don't you ...?	¿Por qué no...?19
why?	¿Por qué? 8
wife	esposa 2
will	voluntad 22
wind	viento 14
window	ventana 3
windy	ventoso 14
wine	vino 4
winter	invierno 9
with	con 7
woman	mujer 2
wonderful	maravilloso 19
word processor	procesador de textos 11
work (n)	trabajo 5
work (v)	trabajar 5
world	mundo 13
worried	preocupado 19
worry (v)	preocuparse 22
Would you like to ...?	¿Quisiera (hacer)...? 15
Would you like..?	¿Quisiera...? 10
wrist	muñeca 19
write (v)	escribir 5

Y

yard	jardín 3
year	año 9
yellow	amarillo 3
yes	sí 1
yesterday	ayer 8
yet	todavía 17
yogurt	yogur 10
you can't miss it	es muy fácil de encontrar 7
you	tu/Ud./Uds 1
young	joven 13
your	tu/su 1
yourself	tu/Ud. mismo 22
yourselves	Uds mismos 22
yuk!	¡puaj! 4